THIS IS A CARLTON BOOK
Published in Great Britain in 2018 by
Carlton Books Limited
20 Mortimer Street
London W1T 3JW

A CIP catalogue for this book is available from the British Library.

Project Editor: Ross Hamilton
Editorial: Caroline Curtis and Chris Stone
Design: Russell Knowles and Natasha Le Coultre
Picture Research: Steve Behan
Production: Yael Steinitz
Index: Colin Hynson

ISBN 978-1-78739-179-6

Printed in Dubai

10 9 8 7 6 5 4 3 2 1

MADONNA

ALBUM BY ALBUM

CAROLINE SULLIVAN

CARLTON
BOOKS

CONTENTS

INTRODUCTION

Previous Pages: As an unknown pop hopeful, 1982, on the eve of becoming the most culturally significant female pop artist in history.

Left: Since the start of her career (here, during the *Like a Virgin* era) Madonna has changed what was considered possible for women in music, running every aspect of her career herself.

Madonna wasn't meant to be an albums artist. When she signed to Sire Records in 1982, she was contracted for just two singles – which wasn't an unreasonable assessment of her prospects. She had come along, this unknown Midwesterner, at the wrong time, making aerated disco music when the mainstream charts were dominated by rock and pop. She may have looked hip and she was certainly ambitious – but her electro/dance sound seemed too niche to make an impact outside Manhattan's disco scene.

Thirty years on, it's easy enough to accuse Sire of lacking vision – just two singles, for heaven's sake? How did it not foresee her success? But it can't really be blamed for misreading the crystal ball. Nobody could have predicted that MTV would become the dominant force for breaking new artists, or that she would expertly harness its powers. Nobody, for that matter, knew that teenage girls were ready to be bowled over by a pop singer who wasn't just sexually voracious but completely unfazed by the idea of society's disapproval. The cultural change she would generate was beyond anybody's powers of prediction.

That said, she wasn't without fans at the label. When her demo tape, a song called 'Everybody', reached A&R manager Michael Rosenblatt in the early spring of 1982, he was intrigued enough to call a meeting. When he met her, he instantly realized the potential of "this girl sitting in my office [who] was just radiating star power". The problem, as he told Sean Howe of *Rolling Stone* 30 years later, was the music itself, which "wasn't amazing". Nonetheless, her ambition impressed him – "I want to rule the world," she cheerily told him – so he passed her demo to label president Seymour Stein.

For his part, Stein professed himself amazed by 'Everybody'. He was being treated for a heart infection, but was so smitten by the song that he summoned her to his hospital room. Madonna arrived that evening, at 8 p.m., incandescent with excitement, having got it into her head that a record deal would be signed there and then.

Major labels don't operate that way, but meeting her in the flesh crystallized things for Stein. Her determination to be a star swayed him to the point that they shook hands on a deal that night. He advised her to find a lawyer, and arranged another meeting for two weeks later, when he would be out of hospital.

His enthusiasm wasn't matched by his bosses. "I was shocked that I had a lot of opposition at Warner Bros [Sire's parent company] from the very top," he told the New York radio station WNYC. "They didn't hear it at all." Stein's gift for talent-spotting was writ all over Sire's roster, in the form of Talking Heads, the Pretenders and the Ramones. Yet in the opinion of Stein's bosses, Warner chairman Mo Ostin and head lawyer David Berman, Madonna and her baby voice and clattery electronic beats didn't have crossover potential. Hence that two-single deal. She signed it in April 1982, when she was 23. Sire got her cheaply – there were no other offers.

Produced by club DJ-turned-producer Mark Kamins, 'Everybody' was essentially a club groove with bleepy synth accents and Madonna's breathy vocal coasting along the top. The self-written lyric was an anodyne appeal to "everybody" to get themselves down to a club and forget their troubles by dancing. (She would return to that theme numerous times on her first few albums.) Sire decided not to use her picture on the sleeve, to foster the impression she was black – that had been the assumption of some punters when the record had been previewed at clubs, and there seemed no reason to reveal the truth, when doing so would have kept the single from being played on R&B radio. Instead, the sleeve used a collage of New York street life – fire hydrant, Lower East Side tenement, kid on roller skates – to suggest that, whoever this Madonna was, she knew her urban signifiers.

After testing well in clubs, including the Paradise Garage (where she later filmed the single's video, rather giving the game away about her racial identity), 'Everybody' was released in October. And Ostin and Berman were right: it didn't go anywhere near the pop chart. However, it's worth noting what she was up against. In the weeks immediately before and after its release, the top singles in the US chart were by the Steve Miller Band, John Cougar and Men at Work, all of them unequivocal meat-and-potatoes rockers. The best-selling single of that whole year was Olivia Newton John's soft-centred 'Physical', and the only other solo women singers in the year-end Top 20 were Joan Jett and Melissa Manchester. The latter's 'You Should Hear How She Talks About You' had a faint disco influence – well, there was a beat – but it was a manicured, vanilla thing when heard alongside Madonna's raw 'Everybody'.

Instead of worrying about the pop chart, Sire concentrated their promotional efforts on clubs and urban radio. The video was sent out with the record, which helped a great deal. When club crowds saw it – a simple clip of her dancing on the Paradise Garage stage in front of a crowd of punters, which had the kind of woozy, Saturday night feel any club audience could relate to – it all made sense. Being able to see Madonna, who emanated charisma even in grainy film clips, was as important as hearing her, and turned out to be key to breaking the record. 'Everybody' reached Number 3 in the dance chart, selling around 100,000 copies.

"I had the radio on in my bedroom, on [dance station] KTU, and I heard 'Everybody'," she told Austin Scaggs of Rolling Stone in 2009. "It was an amazing feeling."

The second single of her Sire deal, 'Burning Up', also missed the mainstream chart when it came out in March 1983, but reached Number 3 on the dance list. (Oddly enough: it was laced with guitar, and not especially danceable.) That decided it for Sire: she was an albums artist after all. The contract was extended, and she began putting together what would become her self-titled first album. With it came a new identity. Talking to American author J. Randy Taraborrelli in the late 90s, Mark Kamins recalled a declaration she'd made when it looked as if things were starting to take off. "The old me was Madonna Louise Ciccone," she told Kamins. "The new me is Madonna."

Right: The recipe for success: sharp pop instincts, a business brain and the kind of sexiness that transgressed what was thought "respectable". More than 300 million album sales later...

She felt it unfair. She didn't have sex until fairly late, and then it was with a long term boyfriend, so there was no foundation to the insults.

Deciding she didn't fit in at school, she threw herself into dance. It had been an interest for several years, ever since she had persuaded her father to let her take ballet classes instead of piano lessons – all the Ciccone offspring were expected to learn a musical instrument. In 10th grade, aged around 16, she met a ballet teacher called Christopher Flynn, who became her mentor, introducing her to the arts scene in nearby Detroit. He took her to galleries and gay clubs, feeding her interest in culture.

The gay scene was a revelation: a place where an assertive nature was a boon for a woman. The main club was called Menjo's, and there she found a spiritual home. Before AIDS, gay nightlife was devoted to free expression and sometimes debauchery; above all, it promoted a policy of being yourself. Madonna's thinking was already running along those lines; dancing at Menjo's was the physical expression of it. "Because I was a really aggressive woman, guys [at school] thought of me as a really strange girl," she said in 1991 to Don Shewey of *The Advocate*, an American gay and lesbian magazine. But at Menjo's, she acquired what she called "a whole new sense of myself."

She was a good enough dancer to win a scholarship to the University of Michigan, but left halfway through her degree for the far brighter lights of New York. She was encouraged by Flynn, who recognized that Detroit had little to offer her. In New York, she would find the bohemianism she craved; from a professional viewpoint, too, the city offered far more potential for a half-trained dancer who was still deciding what she wanted to do with her life.

It was July 1978, a month before her twentieth birthday. She arrived in New York with, according to legend, just $35 and no

Left: Her acting headshot from autumn 1978, after Madonna moved to New York to study dance.

Right Above: Giving it the school spirit, Madonna (top right) with the Rochester Adams High cheerleading squad.

Right Below: Madonna looking sultry modelling in New York, 1978. The sassy/sexy Madonna "look" was beginning to emerge.

contacts. After getting off the plane, she took a taxi to Times Square and then, she claims, wandered along with her suitcase until a passer-by took pity and let her stay in his apartment for two weeks. From there, she moved into a succession of apartments, scraping a living. She was broke much of the time, but saw this as part and parcel of an artistic lifestyle: at 20, she was young enough to view poverty as romantic.

She quickly found her way to the periphery of the city's hipster fraternity. Pre-recessionary, pre-AIDS New York would have been a liberating place: downtown nightlife was boundary-free, with the arts cross-pollinating. She found herself at the nexus of gay and punk culture, socializing with dancers, artists, designers and musicians. She studied dance with Martha Graham and Pearl Lang, making ends meet by working as a waitress and sometime nude model (the pictures would duly surface when she became famous).

It was the quintessential boho life, though she found it hard. In 1984, she told told the *Los Angeles Times*' Robert Hilburn, "I'd go to Lincoln Center, sit by a fountain and just cry. I'd write in my little journal and pray to have even one friend." (Her account was disputed by her older brother, Martin, who told J. Randy Taraborrelli, "Oh, please, she never sat by a fountain and cried. … she had loads of friends.")

At one stage, she landed a gig as a backing dancer for French disco star Patrick Hernandez, then riding the crest of his only hit, 'Born to be Alive'. She went to Paris for the job, and was noticed by his management, who decided that this punky, strikingly attractive American was wasted playing a bit part in the Patrick Hernandez Revue. They promised to develop a singing career for her, and teamed her with producers, but progress was achingly slow. No evidence exists that any recordings were ever made; whatever the case, Madonna lost patience and returned to New York. Apparently, her final words to Hernandez were: "Success is yours today, honey, but it will be all mine tomorrow."

The Hernandez experience did change her game: it shifted her focus from dancing to singing. Shortly after returning from Paris, she met an American musician called Dan Gilroy, with whom she

Previous Pages and Far Left: Looking beautiful and introspective as she gazes into a dressing-room mirror. Spring 1979.

Left: A previously unpublished photograph taken while Madonna was attending the University of Michigan, circa 1976/77.

Below: The emergence of the classic Madonna look from a photoshoot take at Canal Street, Manhattan, December 1982.

became romantically involved. They decided to form a band called the Breakfast Club, with Madonna on drums (as a dancer, she had the requisite rhythmic skills), though she swiftly graduated to lead vocals. The internet has no shortage of Breakfast Club audio clips, which reveal a rudimentary band with a spiky, New Wave guitar sound. The poor recording quality does Madonna's squeaky-but-valiant vocals no favours, but there's an undeniable energy there.

There was something of the early Debbie Harry to her; Harry herself had been in a ramshackle, pre-punk band called the Stilettos (or Stillettos/Stilettoes, depending on who was designing their gig posters), which relied on B-movie campness as much as it did music. By the time Madonna started making music, Harry was the globally renowned singer of Blondie, but she hadn't lost her mix of vulnerability and wry amusement. If Madonna admired any female musician while she was in the Breakfast Club, it was Harry – although, as the British music writer Chris Roberts once said, Harry had "eyes like a wounded kitten," while Madonna's vulnerability was internalized; on the surface, she appeared focused and calculating.

"I was hugely influenced by Debbie Harry when I started out," she once said. "I thought she was the coolest chick in the universe."

Around 1979, a boyfriend from her college days, Steve Bray, moved to New York and joined the Breakfast Club as drummer. After a few months, the band underwent a reconfiguration and became Emmy. The name Madonna had actually wanted was "Madonna", but Bray balked at that: not only was it religious, it suggested the rest of the band were mere sidemen to one particular member. "Is everything about you?" Bray asked her. Years later, he told writer Lucy O'Brien, "I realized far too late that, yes, it is all about you." At that point, however, Bray was the most musically experienced of the band, so she reluctantly agreed to "Emmy".

"I was hugely influenced by Debbie Harry when I started out... I thought she was the coolest chick in the universe." Madonna

Despite getting themselves onto the Manhattan gig circuit, Emmy didn't break through. Even with Madonna as frontwoman, they hadn't yet found their own sound, and the songs needed polishing beyond the band's abilities. In 1980, as she was becoming frustrated with the lack of progress, she met Camille Barbone, owner of a recording studio called Gotham Records. She persuaded Barbone to come to an Emmy gig, and Barbone was impressed enough to offer to manage her – provided she left the band. "She sparkled. It was hard and guttural and in-your-face. She very much typified the New York music scene," she told O'Brien.

Madonna left Emmy without hesitation, and cast her lot with Barbone. Her new manager found her an apartment, gave her an allowance of $100 a week and assembled a backing band, with which Madonna rehearsed new material. Most importantly, perhaps, Barbone was an "in" to the mainstream music industry, introducing her to producers, DJs and industry types that would otherwise have been beyond her reach. Barbone thought she was only a fair musician – though her lyrics weren't bad – but her gift for attracting

23

attention rendered such considerations moot. Onstage, Madonna was the only person anyone noticed; at meetings with industry executives, she won them over by sheer force of personality.

Writing much of the music herself, she made a four-track demo in the summer of 1981. Three of the songs were roughly in line with the pop-rock she'd made with her previous bands; the fourth, 'Get Up', pointed in a different direction, toward the dance music she'd been hearing in the downtown clubs. She found herself at odds with Barbone over the sound, and then about the fact that a record deal had yet to materialize. In February 1982, she terminated their contract – to the latter's great dismay. It took Barbone years to come to terms with seeing her former client achieve global success, but eventually, she told Lucy O'Brien in 2004, she realized that she wouldn't have been able to take Madonna to the next level herself. "I was totally ill-equipped to have that kind of hit. My philosophy now is that it was meant to be."

Meanwhile, Madonna and Steve Bray had been working on music together, independently of Camille, and had come up with a track called 'Everybody'. It was a buzzy synth-dance number, along the same lines as 'Get Up', but much catchier. She was determined to get it heard, and decided to deliver a cassette of it to Mark Kamins, one of the regular DJs at the hipster hangout Danceteria. She was already a regular there, so it was easy enough for her to hand it to him in his DJ booth.

He gave it a spin in the club the next night, and noted that it was a "fun" little tune that got a good response from punters. Soon after that night, she and Kamins became a couple, and he took it upon himself to get her what she wanted most, a record deal. The first label he took the tape to, Island, declined. Next on his list was Sire Records, where he had a connection in the form of A&R manager Michael Rosenblatt. Finally, Madonna was about to make the transition from wannabe to star-in-waiting.

Above and Right: Thought to be among her earliest concert photographs, Madonna fronts the Breakfast Club – at Uncle Sam's Blues Club, Roslyn, Long Island, 1981.

25

CHAPTER 2
MADONNA

*The debut album was inspired by
New York's torrid disco scene, setting
out Madonna's stall as a dance princess.
Effervescent and frankly insubstantial,
it sold 10 million copies, but hardly hinted
at the genre-changing career to come.*

Madonna photographed for *Interview* magazine,
New York, 1982, before the release of 'Everybody'.

MADONNA

Who is this girl with a voice like helium and bracelets made of rubber? Madonna finds her look, makes an album and decides to pursue world domination.

By early 1983, Madonna had had two bona fide dance hits – 'Everybody' and 'Burning Up' – and Sire exercised its option for an album. As producer of 'Everybody', Kamins had expected to be allowed to produce the album. He may have also hoped that being her on-off boyfriend would count for something, but Madonna rarely let sentimentality cloud her vision. (From her earliest days in New York, her relationships were usually short-lived, and often secondary to her career.) Instead, the record company appointed Reggie Lucas, who had produced 'Burning Up'. He was a top R&B name, accustomed to working with artists of the calibre of Lou Rawls and Phyllis Hyman, whereas Kamins was a club DJ and producer who lacked experience in guiding vocalists.

Kamins wasn't the first person to have been cut out of the picture when Madonna met someone better able to help her, but this particularly hurt. It was becoming clear that she was going to be successful, and for Kamins to be ditched for another producer, even a more suitable one, was hard to accept. He was especially dismayed because he'd thought he and Madonna had had an agreement. This informal deal, made before she signed to Sire, had been that if he got her a recording contract, he would have first dibs on producing her debut album – hence his anger at being passed over.

Kamins went on to work with David Byrne and Sinead O'Connor, and eventually moved to Mexico, where he died of a heart attack, aged 57, in 2013. Madonna's response, as printed in the *Hollywood Reporter*, was a characteristic mix of detachment and emotion: "I'm very sorry to hear about Mark's death. I haven't seen him for years but if it weren't for him, I might not have had a singing career. He was the first DJ to play my demos before I had a record deal. He believed in me before anyone else did. I owe him a lot. May he rest in peace."

As Lucas and Madonna began to work together, it became clear that they were an odd couple. His production style was lush (an example is Stephanie Mills' extravagantly pretty 1980 disco hit 'Never Knew Love Like This Before') and hers was sparse. She found it hard to adjust to his way of working, complaining that he layered the sound with multiple instruments and effects. She had her own ideas, which she was keen to try, and she was frustrated not to be allowed to take the lead. He had to explain that his job, as producer, was to shape the album's overall sound, whether she liked it or not.

Essentially, she had an affinity with the hard-edged music being played at the gay, black and punk clubs, and wanted to create her

Right, Top: Madonna in 1982. Photographer Deborah Feingold took this shot in a session that lasted only 20 minutes.

Right: In Europe to promote her debut album, Madonna is photographed on the roof of her record label office, Soho, London, 1983.

> *"He [Kamins]
> believed in me
> before anyone
> else did. I owe
> him a lot."*
>
> Madonna

Left: Madonna's first official UK photoshoot, London, 1983. The photographer Joe Bangay recalled she was "nervous but polite and brilliant".

Right: Already completely comfortable in front of the camera. From the 1982 *Interview* magazine session.

own version. She was inspired by the clubs where she spent three or four hours a night dancing. A regular at Danceteria, the Mudd Club and Paradise Garage, she was listening to everything from early house music to the spiky UK post-punk of the Pop Group to Grace Jones's frigid, fetishy disco anthems. In fact, at one point, she briefly considered emulating Jones' hyper-polished sound.

Lucas, meanwhile, had a jazz and R&B background; his way of making a record involved traditional craftsmanship and instrumentation. He was only starting to find his way around the new technology of Linn drum machines (which he himself programmed on the album) and OB-X synthesizers, so much of the music on the album was made on low-tech guitar, drums and piano.

But, as they settled in at Manhattan's now-defunct Sigma Sound Studios, he was impressed by her dedication. "I must say, Madonna was great to work with in the studio. She really put in the work," he told Chris Williams of *The Atlantic* magazine. He recalled

her "diligence", a quality many artists lack. Diligence, reliability, a willingness to put in grindingly long hours: they're as necessary as talent when it comes to breaking a new act, and iron-willed Madonna was a model of hard work. With some musicians, flakiness comes as standard, but not this one. She turned up on time – often before the other musicians – and was ready to start as soon as she entered the studio, utterly committed to making the record successful.

She'd already written several songs for the album, including

"Madonna was great to work with... She really put the work in." Reggie Lucas

'Lucky Star', while Lucas came up with 'Borderline' and 'Physical Attraction', written specifically to highlight her effervescent delivery. These three set the album's musical tone. Madonna's desire to create a club-friendly album was, for the most part, realized: the sound across the whole record is glittering and synthetic. (The sole exception is 'I Know It', which is built around a chamber-music keyboard riff that prefigured Eurythmics' 'Sweet Dreams (Are Made of This)' by some six months. In the dance floor-happy company of 'Lucky Star' and the rest, it sounds like a New Wave orphan.)

The album was a learning experience for both parties. It was the first time Lucas had used a drum machine and he and Madonna also came up with a mini-Moog bass sound that became one of her standard motifs. Madonna also learned a good deal about phrasing, and playing around with the beat; meanwhile, her knack for improvising is evident in the coolly effective little yeahs and ahhhs that pop up at the end of lines. Her instincts were pretty near unerring – she knew what she needed to do as a vocalist to sell a song.

She also knew how to load lyrics with her conflicting desires. On the one hand, she was a romantic, with a melting marshmallow heart; on the other, a sexually assertive woman. She was "burning up" with physical need, but also grateful for the manly "lucky star" who was her shield against the world. (Sometimes, though, as with 'Everybody', she wasn't in the mood for any romantic interplay, and burned off her sexual energy on an anonymous dance floor.) There was an implicit power exchange: at times, she allows the man to be dominant, while at other times she's the aggressor. The limitations of her voice turn out to be one of her strong suits: her airy little squeaks make her seem deceptively powerless, which turns out to be the album's big joke. Her range and timbre may be small and breathy, but if that makes listeners underestimate her, it's their mistake.

Anthony Jackson, who played bass on 'Borderline', was impressed by her abilities. "I have to give Madonna a lot of credit," he told Lucy O'Brien. "She knows she's not the greatest singer, but she knows how to get the music down." Yet when the studio sessions finished, she wasn't especially happy with the mixes. Her boyfriend at that point was John "Jellybean" Benitez, a radio and club DJ who had exactly

"She knows she's not the greatest singer, but she knows how to get the music down."

Anthony Jackson

the sort of urban-dance ear Madonna was searching for. Benitez ended up remixing several tracks, and producing a new song called 'Holiday', which he came across at the last minute. It had been turned down by Mary Wilson and Phyllis Hyman, but in Madonna's hands became one of the album's highlights – a breezy disco concoction, with one of the most euphoric vocals she ever produced. (The sleeve also credits her with playing "cowbelle" on it.)

Jellybean has complained that although he "sweetened up" some of the music, he didn't get a co-producer's credit other than on 'Holiday'. For his part, Lucas doesn't see Benitez as co-producer, telling *The Atlantic*: "Jellybean produced 'Holiday' and remixed a couple of tracks, but [that] isn't the same thing as producing one of the major breakout pop stars of the 1980s." Over the years, however, the misconception has arisen that Jellybean was the album's main producer – something that frustrates Lucas, who claims that people are surprised when he informs them that in fact it was he who produced the bulk of it.

Lyrically, 'Holiday' was right up Madonna's street, buoyantly asking the entire world to take a day off and celebrate being alive. Most of

Right: With her star on the rise, Madonna poses for the Canal Street photoshoot, New York, 1982.

Overleaf: Sexy, sultry, impish: a contact sheet from the Madonna Canal Street session, 1982.

31 A　　　32　　　32 A　　　33　　　33 A　　　34

ILFORD　　　　　FP4

10 A　　　11　→　11A　　　12　→　12A

FP4　　　　　　　　　　　　　　ILFOF

34A 35 35A 36 36A

ILFORD FP4 SAFETY

13A 14 14A 15 15A

FP4 SAFETY FILM

the record's songs were similarly universal in sentiment. Even in her days with Camille Barbone, she had been an effective lyricist – it was one of the things Barbone had considered most promising, her ability to pen verses that spoke to everyone. She wrote honestly, and with a minimum of frills; her lyrics weren't poetic or complex, but they had an openness to which women in particular could relate.

The album's lyric sheet bears that out. 'Lucky Star', 'I Know It' and 'Think of Me', to take three songs at random: they're about the euphoria of being in love, the pain of discovering that the love is a one-way street, and her determination to walk away before she gets hurt again. There's nothing profound there, but, paired with Reggie Lucas's sparkling arrangements, the songs are greater than the sum of their parts. Lucas and Madonna did the same thing across the whole record, resulting in a release that set the standard for dance-pop for the next 20 years, according to critic Stephen Thomas Erlewine. "It cleverly incorporated great pop songs with stylish, state-of-the-art beats... a showcase for a dynamic lead singer," he wrote on AllMusic.com.

The self-titled album (it would be re-released in 1985 as *Madonna: The First Album*) was released on July 27, 1983, a few weeks before her twenty-fifth birthday. Just eight tracks long (a 2001 reissue would flesh it out with bonus versions of 'Everybody' and 'Lucky Star'), it was a gleaming, confident introduction to a singer who was still unknown outside the clubs. Although now considered one

of the premier pop records of the 80s, initial reviews were mixed. *Rolling Stone* noted that her voice "takes some getting used to", while the influential American critic Robert Christgau was both charmed and irked by her "shamelessly ersatz sound" (but liked it enough, on balance, to award it an A-).

Critically speaking, it has fared better with the benefit of hindsight, with reviewers today praising it as a pop game-changer. It's now recognized as the record, that, along with Michael Jackson's *Thriller*, paved the way for dance music, which has dominated the charts ever since. In 2013, *Rolling Stone* adjudged it one of the Top 100 debut albums of all time: "...it didn't just succeed in introducing the most important female voice in the history of modern music, it's also aged much better sonically than *Like a Virgin*." Reassessing the album on its thirtieth anniversary in 2013, Matthew Lindsay of *The Quietus* agreed: "Her first album remains one of her best works, the supposed 'lack of variety' actually giving it a consistency and focus". (Madonna herself, meanwhile, is surprisingly disparaging, calling it "the aerobics album".)

Back in 1983, it took over a month to dent the chart, creeping in at Number 190 in early September. To chivvy it into life, Sire released 'Holiday' as a single that same week in September. Records took far longer to enter the chart in those days; for an untested act like Madonna, it was a laborious process of getting the music onto radio

and MTV playlists, and hoping listeners would like what they heard. The process could be helped along by one-off gigs and other promotion, but it could take weeks to build the momentum that would finally push a single or album into the chart.

In the case of 'Holiday', it took almost two months, but it gave her the mainstream hit she needed, peaking at Number 16 on the pop chart (and Number 1 on the dance chart). It was a pivotal point, the moment when America noticed her and decided it was interested. With 'Holiday', her sound and image coalesced; her ragamuffin/ hipster look and sexy but curiously wholesome music marked her out as a different kind of star.

(The video for 'Holiday', oddly enough, was never officially released. It's a curio worth searching for on the internet: it was filmed in one bare room, on a budget of – at a guess – $20, and features Madonna and two dancers, one of them her brother Christopher, gyrating to the song. Its starkness gives no hint that Madonna was a priority act, but one thing stands out: she exudes the same energy as if it had been a million-dollar extravaganza. She's clad head-to-toe in what was beginning to be recognized as "Madonna's style", incorporating a fishnet cropped top, rubber bangles and a miniskirt worn over knee-length dancers' leggings. Her dip-dyed blonde-brown hair is straggly, her shoes flat. Dancing up to the camera, she looks right into the lens, revelling in the attention.)

By contrast, her previous video, for 'Burning Up', had been a chewier affair. It started with Madonna kneeling in a road, arching her back in ecstatic anticipation as a man drives a car toward her. There were close-ups of her lips, and of a dog-chain being tightened around her neck, imparting a fetishistic quality; here was a woman in such transports of lust that she was happy to be run over. But in the very last frame, the man has disappeared and she is driving the car, glancing at the camera in an attitude of casual triumph. The video masterfully harnessed her two definitive qualities: her sexual side, which explosively spills over in a way previously unseen in videos by women, and her need to be in charge.

"Capitalizing on her own body, she was both feminine and feminist," wrote Tara Gutman. "She was instantly sexual. She sang about urgent desires rather than goosebumps." By way of a contrasting (and rather isolated) view, Cristian Gonzales of the longstanding fan-site MadonnaTribe.com feels people make too much of the "feminist" angle. "I've always rolled my eyes at such analysis because I seriously doubt Madonna was thinking to herself when she made the video: 'Hmmm...what feminist metaphor do I wish to use here

Above Left: As captured by Deborah Feingold in the photographer's 1982 shoot. Madonna was "shy" while posing.

Above Right: Always happy to try new styles and looks, Madonna wears a leather cap for this 1982 shoot.

in order to confirm that I am a strong woman?' Madonna was just trying to have fun, that's all, open and shut case."

While it's a little simplistic to ascribe the video's imagery to her simply wanting to have a laugh, there's something to his analysis. In 1983, Madonna was probably operating instinctively, rather than according to feminist theory. Commanding by nature, and never beholden to boyfriends (whom she left as soon as she decided a romance had run its course), she would have undoubtedly enjoyed the concept of 'Burning Up'. It makes a feature of her appetites, giving her exhibitionistic streak full reign, as she hungers openly for a physical connection – but just as her oddly robotic boyfriend starts to believe she belongs to him, she flips the script. Off she drives, and we never find out what happens to him.

But to think she was making a statement – beyond "I'm powerful and carnal" – is probably wrong. Madonna was wholly aware of her power, but at that point probably didn't see it as something that would become a lightning rod for Western female sexuality in the late twentieth century. At that stage, she was simply struggling to get established, devoting her energies to the unglamorous nuts-and-bolts of record promotion.

In fact, it was Cyndi Lauper, briefly her arch-rival, who was making overtly feminist anthems: 'Girls Just Want to Have Fun', coincidentally released on the same day as 'Holiday', was a celebration of female self-expression, and of saying no to authority. Accompanied by a video using then-new computer imagery, it became a far bigger hit than 'Holiday', peaking at Number 2 and making Lauper America's biggest new pop star. Until Madonna overtook her with the *Like a Virgin* album, it seemed as if Lauper would be the greater overall success.

Madonna's supreme self-belief marked a new kind of female pop archetype. She insisted that her ideas be given equal consideration in the studio – even before she knew what she was doing – and she was unshakeable in her convictions. (This was why she refused to give the vastly more experienced Reggie Lucas free rein.) Though she admitted to using feminine wiles when she thought they would help, the notion of letting a man overrule her final decisions was simply inconceivable.

Industry figures who encountered her during this period were struck by her confidence, which could come across as chilliness. The album's art director, Carin Goldberg, admired her directness but was bemused that there was no pretence of friendship. Years later, she recalled Madonna's directness; it was clear that, to her, this was a business relationship only. British journalist Sandy Robertson, who met her during an early UK promo trip, also noted that she was "friendly but reserved".

Talking to *The Face* magazine a year or so later, Madonna was almost preternaturally self-assured. Asked why she admired Marilyn Monroe – a great favourite of hers, along with Carole Lombard and Judy Holliday – she replied: "Her innocence and her sexuality and her humour and her vulnerability." The interviewer informed her that she herself had those qualities, and she said: "I know."

There was no false modesty or disingenuousness – she was simply endowed with the unshakeable belief that she was pretty damned great. Some friends, however, believed she was more vulnerable than she appeared, with an unnamed ex-boyfriend telling *The Face*: "She's deeply terrified of herself and of being alone with herself. Yet she's a much more interesting person than she knows." But what mattered in terms of selling herself was how she was perceived – and the perception was that she was a strong, resourceful woman.

Her strength was always tempered, though, with girlish sweetness. Don't forget that all the songs on the Madonna album were about boys or having a twirl on the dance floor, a combination that made her immensely popular with young girls. Just as important to the fans was her style, which was both quirky and easy to copy. The look was a joint effort between Madonna and one of her Lower East Side clubbing friends, Maripol. A jewellery designer by trade, the French-born Maripol used found objects in her collections, resulting in one-of-a-kind items such as rubber bracelets made out of typewriter belts. Madonna had already developed a thrown-together look that was part-punk, part-thrift-shop and Maripol's ideas chimed well. The

"Madonna went further than any other woman in gleefully deploying the video format to shock, entrance and manipulate viewers."

Andi Zeisler

crucifix earrings she often wore were from the designer's collection, and the look on the cover of the *Madonna* album – bracelets layered upon bracelets – was also Maripol's work.

The video to 'Lucky Star' (her fifth single, released in 1984) crystallized the Madonna Look. She wore an all-black outfit and accessories, with red lipstick the only touch of colour, and her silhouette looked seared into the video set's plain white background. This was the video that turned teenage girls into Wannabes (as in "I wannabe Madonna"). The fingerless gloves, scarf in her hair and black sunglasses were different from what other pop stars were wearing, and if she wasn't the first one to dress this way (Chrissie Hynde wore those gloves on the cover of the first Pretenders album, the Slits often tied their hair with scarves, and sunglasses were a longstanding punk leitmotif), Madonna was the first to mix them all together.

What made the look so attractive was its artlessness: as if she had thrown on the first things she found when she got up that morning. It helped that, despite being 25, she looked much younger – her looks and style had more of the teenage scruff than the grown woman about them.

Meanwhile, the leggings, ballet slippers and leg warmers referenced her dance background, and the red lipstick and heavy eye-makeup were a cheeky nod to mainstream femininity. She was provocative, but innocently, sweetly so. The whole package was enormously attractive to young girls. Before Madonna, they had had few alluring role models: Chrissie Hynde and Pat Benatar were rock chicks, Debbie Harry unattainably gorgeous, Cyndi Lauper a bit too quirky. Meanwhile, America's rigidly formatted radio system ensured that R&B singers like Gwen Guthrie (who sang backing vocals on the Madonna album) and Teena Marie got little mainstream exposure. Hence Madonna.

Once the Wannabes were on board, things began to happen quickly. 'Lucky Star' reached Number 4, and the album began its climb up the chart, finally reaching a peak of Number 8 in October, 1984 – a full 14 months after release. It would go on to sell 10 million copies worldwide.

MTV's role in all this can't be overstated; by 1984, the three-year-old video channel had become a major tool in record promotion, and pop stars didn't get more MTV-friendly than Madonna. She and her video directors understood what was needed. As writer Andi Zeisler noted, "She went further than any other woman in gleefully deploying the video format to shock, entrance and manipulate viewers."

Left: This was a daring look for its time.
From the 1982 Tom Morillo session.

'Borderline', the first video many fans would have seen, exemplifies Zeisler's words. (Released before 'Lucky Star', the song had reached Number 10.) In the video, Madonna plays a home girl, hanging around on a street corner with her Latin boyfriend and his breakdancing friends. She is then swept off her feet by a suave British photographer, and is seen sipping champagne with him to toast her newfound fame. But she finds herself missing her Hispanic boyfriend's virile charms; she dumps the photographer – spray-painting his car as a kiss-off – and returns to the boyfriend. On the surface, it's an everyday story of temptation being overcome by true love (or lust), but it attracted a good deal of cultural commentary.

Much of it focused on the two male archetypes – effete white man, macho Latino – and the way the video reinforces those stereotypes. In that context, the song's lyric, which had Madonna refusing to be a "prisoner" and demanding to be released, was taken as "rebellion against the chauvinistic ways of the Latino," according to Santiago Fouz-Hernandez. But her painting the car was a rejection of the photographer, too: "One could read [it]... as a triumph of the Hispanic..."

The feminist writer Camille Paglia argued that the clip had a more personal meaning. It was about Madonna herself and how she was dealing with the changes in her life. She was on the cusp between her old, funky street-life and significant stardom. In particular, the video addressed the fact that she'd dated many black and Hispanic men, but now she was about to cross the fame threshold, where many doors would be closed to them. The video, wrote Paglia, showed "the new dualities of her life: the gritty, multi-racial street... and her new slick, fast world of popularity and success."

It's hard to say whether Madonna would have gone so far, so fast, if video itself hadn't existed. For all its musical strengths, the debut album took off only once people had seen the clips and realized there was more to her than just chrome-plated beats and a bubbly voice. Madonna herself has disparaged the album: "The songs were pretty weak, and I went to England during the recordings, so I wasn't around. I didn't realise how crucial it was for me to break out of the disco mould... I wish I could have got a little more variety there."

"It just took a long time for people to pay attention to me – and I thank God they did!" Madonna

Yet the record frequently turns up on Best Albums of the 80s lists, and even Madonna has softened her stance recently. "I think it stands up well," she told *Rolling Stone*. "It just took a long time for people to pay attention to me – and I thank God they did!"

That "thank God they did!" makes her sound atypically modest, as if she believed things could easily have gone the other way. She probably never believed that for a minute. Consider her appearance, in January 1984, on the venerable music show *American Bandstand*. Before performing 'Holiday', she did a brief interview with host Dick Clark, who asked whether she'd had any doubts about leaving her previous bands to go solo. "Not really," she replied in a Midwestern twang whose edges had yet to be sanded down by success. "I think I've always had a lot of confidence in myself." What were her intentions for 1984, Clark pressed. Without hesitation, she replied: "To rule the world."

Right: Madonna's self-titled debut album was released on July 27, 1983, a few weeks before her 25th birthday.

CHAPTER 3
LIKE A VIRGIN

Thanks to Nile Rodgers's sparkling production, five blockbuster singles and an iconic belt buckle, Madonna's breakthrough album found a place in 21 million households. Boy Toy or ferociously smart cookie? The jury was out...

An iconic high-glamour shot, 1985.
The trend-setting crucifix earrings and
rubber bracelets are just out of frame.

LIKE A VIRGIN

Like a Virgin makes Madonna an icon, establishing her as a new breed of feminist. Parents are scandalized, the media are fascinated and the Wannabes buy 21 million copies.

The sleeve notes for the *Like a Virgin* album reveal how far Madonna had come from her debut. In the column headed "Xtra special thanks" (as opposed to the plain old "Special thanks", just above it), there are four dedications. Benitez, whom she was still dating, gets a mention, as do her family and her new manager, Freddy DeMann. But the biggest tip of the hat is reserved for the album's producer, at the top of the list. Madonna wrote: "Nile 'Boom' Rodgers: I knew him before the butter dripped off his noodle."

From the tone, she was now in the driver's seat, or at least the co-driver's. Rodgers had produced the album, but it was clear that her relationship with him was one of creative partner, rather than the teacher/student dynamic she'd had with Reggie Lucas. As for his noodle, that's never really been explained, but it was probably Madonna being provocative for the hell of it. Cheeky titillation was a large part of her arsenal at that stage; she was naughty in a cute, Daisy Dukeish way – promising more than she delivered, but always keeping sex on the agenda.

Rodgers was red hot in early 1984, having just produced David Bowie's *Let's Dance* album and INXS's international hit 'Original Sin'. He had been aware of Madonna since seeing her at a small club gig a year earlier and being struck by her star power; she, meanwhile, had idolized him since his days as Chic's songwriter/guitarist. His work on *Let's Dance* would have made him even more desirable in

her eyes: it was Bowie's most successful album to date, certifying that Rodgers was on a hot streak. It was obvious that bringing the two together would yield something special, so Sire was persuaded to pay Rodgers's fee, and in April, producer and artist checked into New York's Power Station studios.

But before that – in January – she went to London to sing 'Holiday' on *Top of the Pops*, her first UK television performance. 'Holiday' had just entered the British chart, and the UK division of Sire had got her onto two pop shows: *Top of the Pops* and Channel 4's flagship "youth" programme, *The Tube*. It was *The Tube* that made the greatest impression. Her performance was filmed not at the show's Newcastle studio but at Manchester's modish Hacienda Club, in front of a gaggle of Mancunian trendies. *The Tube*'s producer, Malcolm Gerrie, has claimed that Sire, not seeing her as a priority act, wouldn't fund her travel from London to Manchester, so the programme paid for the train.

It turned out to be a pivotal moment in her conquest of the world outside America, though there are conflicting reports as to whether it was a triumph on the actual night. A 21-year-old Norman Cook, later famous as Fatboy Slim, was there, and remembered it years later as "mesmerizing", but Mike Pickering, who went on to form M People, thought she was terrible. He told James Nice, "She was really bitchy and I think that transmitted to the audience" – who

Left: Onstage at Madison Square Garden, New York, in June 1985, during her debut arena jaunt, the Virgin Tour.

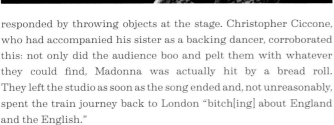

responded by throwing objects at the stage. Christopher Ciccone, who had accompanied his sister as a backing dancer, corroborated this: not only did the audience boo and pelt them with whatever they could find, Madonna was actually hit by a bread roll. They left the studio as soon as the song ended and, not unreasonably, spent the train journey back to London "bitch[ing] about England and the English."

Nevertheless, it was a breakthrough moment. *The Tube* had a large hipster audience who were in thrall to the dance music emanating from across the Atlantic. They viewed Madonna as a significant new addition to the canon, and these opinion-formers got the ball rolling. It didn't hurt that her fashion sense, which by then extended to oversized neon sweaters and graffiti-patterned skirts, sprang from a similar DIY mindset to the British post-punk look. The band Bananarama – who, like Madonna, teetered on the cusp between hipness and mass-market acceptance – typified the Brit version: teased hair, oversized "Buffalo Gal" hats, school-uniform jumpers.

The hipster elite would gradually drift away, supplanted by young pop fans, who discovered her via Radio 1 and magazines like *Smash Hits*. But the uptake by teenage girls took some time; there was a lot of home-grown competition for their pop pound, such as the aforesaid Bananarama, and Kim Wilde, who won the 1983 Brit award

for Best Female Artist. And there was no UK version of MTV to get the video message across, so she wasn't an immediate hit. 'Holiday' did eventually reach Number 2, and her debut album, released in early 1984, Number 6. But it would be years before Madonna truly comprehended the British temperament, and then mainly as a result of marrying a Londoner – Guy Ritchie – and moving to England.

Back in early 1984, however, she was dedicating herself to making *Like a Virgin*. Sire had signed her for only two albums, and this one had to prove her long-term value. Her first instinct was to produce it herself, or at least to play a large part in the production. Disappointed by the experience with Reggie Lucas, she was keen to see her ideas through without having to filter them through someone else. Unsurprisingly, Sire deemed her too inexperienced (she got a co-production credit, along with Steve Bray, for 'Into the Groove', although the song – from the soundtrack to her first film, *Desperately Seeking Susan* – wasn't included on the original version of the album). Madonna complained that Sire's parent company, Warner's, was patriarchal and treated her "like this sexy little girl" – but whatever its shortcomings, the label was canny enough to approve her choice of Nile Rodgers.

He didn't come cheaply; after his success with Bowie, he was confident that he could craft a massive hit for Madonna, and priced

himself accordingly. He assured Sire that *Like a Virgin* would sell 5 million copies, which seemed astronomical, given that her debut had sold only half a million at that point. In return, he negotiated a deal that included both an upfront fee and "points" (extra payments linked to sales). It was, he told Mike Diver in 2013, one of the biggest production deals ever struck, and because the record eventually sold 21 million, he made "a huge amount of money".

Rodgers's ability to think outside generic boxes has seen him hailed as one of popular music's great producers. That's what he did for Madonna: rather than attempting to turn her into a diva, he played to her strengths. She was, as he told Diver, "cute and fabulous and full of life", so he brought that to the fore. But he also ramped up the musicianship, bringing in Chic's Bernard Edwards – the bassist's bassist, responsible for the much-sampled bassline on Chic's 'Good Times' – and drummer Tony Thompson. The result was a sparkling dance-pop hybrid – knowing, flirtatious pop songs propelled by the tautest rhythm section in the business. Rodgers more or less reinvented disco for *Like a Virgin*, and it's regarded as one of the major records of the 80s.

This time around, Madonna benefited from a distinct change in the American pop landscape. Though completed in the late spring of 1984, *Like a Virgin* wasn't released until November, mainly because the debut was still selling ('Holiday', 'Borderline' and 'Lucky Star' hit the singles charts in '84, one after another, each climbing higher than the last). When the album finally appeared, it was at the end of a year in which dance-pop had ruled the LP chart. For 37 weeks that year, the Number 1 slot had been occupied by either Michael Jackson's *Thriller* or Prince's *Purple Rain*, which between them crowded out everything else except Bruce Springsteen, the *Footloose* soundtrack and Huey Lewis. This was a whole different kettle of chart action from 1983, when the biggest albums (apart from *Thriller*, again) were mainly rock. In the new dance-influenced climate, *Like a Virgin* fit right in.

The debut had introduced the perennial Madonna motifs of sexual and social equality. *Like a Virgin* took those ideas and ran with them. The woman revealed on the singles 'Material Girl' and the title track

---

Opposite Right and Left: Turning underwear into outerwear at Radio City Music Hall, New York, in 1985 toward the end of the Virgin Tour.

Above: Now a global superstar, Madonna dancing (with brother Christopher Ciccone) on a German television show in 1984.

Overleaf: Fishnet top, crucifix, rubber bracelets and all: The "look" that is synonymous with Madonna's *Like a Virgin* and one that launched a million Wannabes.

"It's because I haven't found many [female friends] who are worldly wise and intelligent."

Madonna

(neither of which she wrote) was almost a caricature: self-absorbed, self-motivated and hard-faced. On 'Material Girl', she even unfurled a cod-English accent: for her, it was all about appearances – surface rather than substance.

She once said that, as a young girl, she had shamelessly used feminine wiles to get her way with her father; here, she used them to wangle financial security and love. Another track, 'Dress You Up' (also composed by outside writers), was directed at a man whose main appeal seemed to be his bank balance – he had enough cash to wear custom-tailored clothes and afford unspecified "luxuries".

Oddly, 'Dress You Up' invoked the attentions of the Parents' Music Resource Center, the censorship group of the 80s and 90s, which was headed by Al Gore's wife, Tipper. Singling it out for its supposedly inflammatory sexual content, the PMRC added it to the so-called Filthy Fifteen, a list of mid-80s songs deemed exceptionally vulgar or violent. Others on the list were Vanity's 'Strap-on "Robbie Baby"' and WASP's 'Animal (Fuck Like a Beast)', compared to which 'Dress You Up' was supremely inoffensive. Its allusions to sex were so mild that it was closer in feel to the swooniness of a 1960s girl group ditty. Nonetheless, Gore called Madonna "morally bankrupt", and PMRC co-founder Susan Baker accused her of teaching young girls to behave like "porn queens in heat", an overreaction that seems even madder nearly 30 years later.

For some reason, the PMRC was fine with the rest of the album, not even taking offence at the word "virgin". Indeed, the high-powered Gore and Baker may even have had a sneaking admiration for the track 'Over and Over', a motivational message to young women to not let anyone stop them from getting what they want. It's a remarkable song, in which Madonna laughs off criticism from a boyfriend who can't handle her pursuit of success. She slaps him away like a mosquito, declaring that she'll do whatever it takes to get where she wants to be.

"She is in charge of the discourse," said the academic Keith E. Clifton. He was specifically referring to 'Material Girl', but also neatly captured the essence of the album. With this album, she was almost recasting female roles – or rather, the role of one particular female: herself. At that point, she didn't seem interested in being a

Above: Madonna onstage in 1985 at Madison Square Garden with her support act, the then-unknown Beastie Boys.

Right: The material girl, bejewelled at an aftershow party at The Palladium, New York, June 1985.

gender role model. She wasn't even a girls' girl, telling *Smash Hits* in February 1984 that she had few female friends. "It's because I haven't found many who are worldly wise and intelligent," she claimed, adding that she preferred the company of "boys" – presumably because boys responded so gratifyingly to her come-hither persona, while women were more sceptical.

Accordingly, many feminists had a hard time with her, even before they removed the shrink-rap from the record. The sleeve photo showed Madonna personifying the virgin/whore dichotomy by wearing a wedding dress (cut low enough so it barely contains her bosom) and white lace gloves, offset by a belt labelling her, in two-inch-high metal letters, a "Boy Toy". The belt was the most inflammatory piece of kit in her entire wardrobe, and even Madonna seemed taken aback by the reaction it caused. She countered that "Boy Toy" was simply a nickname she'd been given when she arrived in New York, and she'd had it made into a belt because that had been the fashion at the time. (eBay currently sells Boy Toy belts as part of a "Madonna-style fancy-dress costume", which also includes a white basque, net skirt and crucifix necklace. All for just £26.99: one generation's incendiary device is another's costume-party accessory.)

Once the record was on the turntable (or in the CD player – it was one of the first to be available in the compact disc format), there

Above Left: Performing in 35˚C heat in front of nearly 100,000 people at the Philadelphia Live Aid concert.

Above and Previous Pages: "I was never elected homecoming queen, but I feel like one now," she said during the Virgin show.

Opposite Above: Madonna onstage at Madison Square Garden in 1985, looking like a bride during one of the set's many costume changes.

were the outta-my-way mission statements disguised as pop songs. Many saw her as part and parcel of the out-for-yourself Reagan era; she was perceived as greedy and materialistic. There was no obvious spiritual dimension to the album, no Cyndi Lauperish sisterliness. *Ms* magazine, then America's highest-profile feminist publication, named Lauper one of its women of the year in 1985, but entirely ignored Madonna.

The singer herself, though, refused to accept the criticism. She denied being "anti-feminist", claiming that her success, which she'd won on her own terms, was proof she was pro-woman. And, to be fair, she pioneered a business model that many other female artists have subsequently followed. Before Madonna, few women in pop openly called the shots in their careers; the important decisions were usually made by their managers and labels. Her toughness and independence changed that. It's now routine for women musicians to exercise control, or at least to say they do – it's no coincidence that Janet Jackson's 1986 breakthrough album, released as Madonna was reaching the apex of her superstardom, was called *Control*.

As with the debut, reviews were mixed. *The New York Times'* Stephen Holden was ambivalent, praising it as "this year's definitive model of danceable urban teen-pop" but noting that she was "the brassiest singer... that [has] been spawned by music video"; Robert Christgau applauded her brazenness in "selling herself as a sex fantasy" but was less sold on the music itself, which he decided wasn't quite as tuneful as the debut.

Critics in the twenty-first century see things a bit differently. The modern consensus is that while it lacks the splashy joie de vivre of the first album – "overall, [*Like a Virgin*] adds up to less than the sum of its parts," wrote AllMusic.com's Steven Thomas Erlewine – it's an indubitable cultural landmark. The "boy toy" and "material girl" personas are seen as ironic send-ups of their era, and the first two singles ('Like a Virgin' and 'Material Girl') regarded as transformational pop moments. All told, it's now fêted as the launch pad that blasted her from starlet to icon.

She and Rodgers managed to finish the album in a couple of months, but – much to her frustration – its release was delayed to let the debut album finish its cycle. It sold its millionth copy in August 1984, a few days before her twenty-sixth birthday. (Media coverage of the time often reported her age as a couple of years younger, and even now it's hard to believe that she was closer to 30 than 20. Much of her allure had to do with the idea that she was a saucy young thing, rather than a mature woman approaching her late twenties.)

Her impatience with the delay was partly due to her belief that the album would lead to film roles. That other curvaceous, often-underrated blonde Marilyn Monroe had been an idol since childhood, and Madonna's desire to act was surely linked to having watched

Left: Playing a nightclub singer
in the 1985 film *Vision Quest*
– her first appearance in a
major motion picture.

Monroe's films and realizing that acting was the ultimate show-off profession. Music, she had discovered, wasn't so different from acting – as a singer, she was enacting a role – but she also wanted to do the real thing, on the big screen. From there, she envisaged directing her own films. Music videos were a kind of trial run, their storylines letting her test herself as an actress, but by 1984, she was ready to move on to actual films.

There had already been a cameo as a nightclub singer in the coming-of-age drama *Vision Quest*. But that appearance – in which she sang 'Crazy for You' and 'Gambler' (both recorded expressly for the film soundtrack, and not available on any studio album) – was essentially a promotional tool for her music. Her next crack at the movies involved proper acting: it was the role of Susan in *Desperately Seeking Susan*. This turned out to be exactly the sort of Hollywood vehicle she was looking for. Nominally, its star was Rosanna Arquette, but by the time it came out, in March 1985, Madonna's celebrity had eclipsed Arquette's, and the perception was that Madonna was the star. Which she wasn't; Arquette got far more screen time, but the misconception was so widespread that when Arquette received a 1986 Bafta Award, it was for Best Actress in a Supporting Role.

Filming began in September 1984, with Susan Seidelman directing, and a cast packed with Manhattan music scenesters, including Richard Hell, John Lurie and Annie Golden. Madonna played a vagabondish free spirit, and Arquette a housewife who gets caught up in her life. The two women had a physical resemblance, which made the mistaken-identities plot plausible: you could have easily mistaken Arquette for Madonna, especially when both were decked out in "Susan's" hair-bows and jewellery.

The role didn't really stretch her – as cute, breezy Susan, she was more or less playing herself – but she received encouraging reviews. The warmest were those that lumped her and Arquette together as a double act. Roger Ebert of the *Chicago Sun-Times* lauded "the special appeal that Arquette and Madonna are able to generate... they somehow succeed in creating specific, interesting characters." *The New York Times'* venerated Vincent Canby went further than that, writing, "Miss Arquette and Madonna are delights" – which was tantamount to being anointed the Next Big Acting Thing.

Taken on her own merits, however, she generated lukewarm reviews. Some critics allowed that, for a fledgling actress, she wasn't too bad; *Variety* pointedly noted that Arquette "does more than her share". That seems unfair, as Madonna was highly watchable, and the film did pave the way for more acting work, as she had hoped. But Canby's endorsement failed to work much magic. None of her subsequent films, with the exception of *Evita*, has ever been as critically successful, and her essays into directing have not been well received.

There was, however, one element of the film that everyone loved: the soundtrack song 'Into the Groove'. It was the most immediate tune she had ever recorded up to that point, an insanely catchy command to join her on the dance floor. As the self-written lyric has it, dancing is both a courtship ritual and a curative activity that can be practised alone – in your room at home, if it comes to that. Combined with production by herself and Steve Bray, which made lavish use of synths and overdubs, it was the kind of confection ABBA would have written, encased in a 1980s chromium shell.

A Madonna song on which everything from voice to drum machines gels perfectly, it continues to be one of her best loved. A perennial American radio favourite, it has popped up on myriad Best Of lists, from *Blender* magazine's 500 Greatest Songs Since You Were Born to *Slant* magazine's 100 Greatest Dance Songs. In 1989, *Billboard* named it Dance Single of the Decade, a notable accolade in a decade that had also produced Prince's '1999', Jackson's 'Billie Jean' and even New Order's 'Blue Monday'. Oddly, it was never released as a single in America. Because it wasn't on *Like a Virgin*, Sire didn't have it scheduled as a single, and was concerned that if they did release it, it would siphon sales away from the next "official" single, 'Angel'. As a compromise, it eventually appeared as the B-side to 'Angel'. In Britain, it was released in its own right, shot to Number 1 and became the biggest UK hit of her career, with 860,000 sales.

In September, she began the second album's promotional campaign by appearing at the inaugural MTV Video Music Awards. She was nominated for Best New Artist (that gong was won by Eurythmics), and also performed. The show's director had expected her to sing one of her hits, but she insisted on premiering 'Like a Virgin', which wouldn't be

released for another two months. Given the opportunity to rope in a large TV audience, she rose to the occasion. The song started with her atop a large wedding cake, wearing a wedding gown, veil and Boy Toy belt. An impassive "groom" stood next to her – but she soon left him, descending the tiers of the cake and pulling back the veil to reveal her face. Three minutes of sultry slinking followed, her delivery becoming progressively more suggestive. She tossed the veil away, pulling her hair out of its prim bun – "Why, Miss Ciccone, you're beautiful!" – and then, consumed by a bride's passion, rolled on the floor, revealing white suspenders and knickers.

Judging by the volume of the applause that greeted this, the audience was bemused rather than ecstatic. As with many things Madonna, hindsight has put a much more favourable spin on the performance. Decades later, MTV's Jocelyn Vena remembered it as one of the most "iconic" moments ever hosted by the channel. She suggested that Lady Gaga, nominated for multiple awards that year, would have to put on quite a show to beat Madonna's 25 years before. That three minutes in 1984, she argued, was the point when Madonna became a superstar.

The performance certainly challenged the idea that a wedding dress denoted purity. The writhing on the floor, on top of all that, was considered downright shocking by some viewers, not least her then-

manager, Freddy DeMann. As Madonna recalled in 2012 on *The Tonight Show* with Jay Leno, DeMann had told her: "That's it, you've ruined your career." She was unruffled. "Since I didn't really have a career yet, I didn't feel I'd lost anything." Anyway, she added, she hadn't planned to roll on the stage; she'd lost one of her stiletto heels while descending the tiers of the cake and had simply dropped to the floor to grab it.

This was America's introduction to the new album, and the new high-concept Madonna. In the short term, she stole the evening, which was supposed to have been dominated by seven-times-nominated Cyndi Lauper. In the longer term, it put paid to any lingering idea that she was a disposable disco starlet. She was now on a different level, preparing for take-off.

The 'Like a Virgin' single was released in October, followed two weeks later by the album. Despite her misgivings about the five-month delay between recording and release, the timing couldn't have been better. Fortuitously, the debut album had just been certified double platinum (2 million copies sold), while at the same time the 'Lucky Star' single was

Above: Her dynamic show, performed with a band and two backing dancers, proved she was no Boy Toy.

Right: Provocation was her watchword, as proved by this 1985 pose in *People* magazine.

"She will be a force to be reckoned with."

Mary Edgar Smith, Atlanta Journal-Constitution

just reaching its highest chart position, Number 4. In essence, she was ubiquitous. Accordingly, *Like a Virgin* hit the charts running. Within two months, it was double platinum, while the title track hit the Number 1 spot in the US singles chart and stayed there for six weeks. (In the UK, the album topped the chart and the single reached Number 3.)

The video for 'Like a Virgin', partly filmed in Venice with a real lion as her co-star, outclassed all her previous efforts in terms of production values. Directed by Mary Lambert, it could be considered a fantasy – camera shots jumped from Madonna looking like a princess in her wedding dress to Madonna wearing lycra and dancing in a gondola – or taken as something deeper. There were two lions in the video: the real one (which terrified her by wandering up during a take and roaring in her face) and a man in a lion mask, playing her bridegroom. Meanwhile, she herself played both a bride, carried off by her new husband, and a wanton hussy, bumping and grinding in the gondola.

Whatever it meant, the effect was dreamy and erotic. Taken in tandem with the song itself, it was seen by conservatives as an attack on morality. Her influence on teenage girls was already manifesting itself in the new fashion for cropped tops, leggings and T-shirts with the legend "Virgin". Now she appeared to be undermining marriage.

Family values campaigners, however, quickly discovered that the Ma-genie was now out of the bottle, and there was no going back. It was just too easy for young girls to fall in love with someone who not only ran her own career but was so dizzyingly transgressive: she made "trashy" clothes look cool, and glamorized the idea of sexual freedom. She conducted sex and relationships on mutually agreed terms, an attitude that empowered the mid-80s generation of girls.

Her next video, for 'Material Girl', showed that hollowness and artifice could be just as effective as organic sincerity. It was a pastiche of Marilyn Monroe in *Gentlemen Prefer Blondes*, right down to the pink gown Monroe wore when she sang 'Diamonds are a Girl's Best Friend'.

As in the film, Madonna surrounded herself with dinner-jacketed hunks – but where Monroe flirted and exerted her femininity for their benefit, Madonna virtually ignored her posse of male dancers. They were there to highlight her, not the other way around.

There's a certain irony in the fact that she found love during the shoot. In December 1984, she broke up with Jellybean, with whom she'd maintained a two-year open relationship. They had been engaged for part of that time, according to Jellybean, but both had seen other people during their time together, and Jellybean had worried that she wouldn't be monogamous if they ever married. Shortly after they split, she met Sean Penn – on the set of 'Material Girl', again directed by his friend Mary Lambert. He was 24, and his acting career was on the up; Madonna had seen some of his films, which included *Fast Times at Ridgemont High* and *Racing with the Moon*, and admired him. He in turn was intrigued by her, and asked Lambert to engineer a meeting.

The chemistry was immediate. They began dating, and were married just seven months later. The ceremony, in Malibu, California, on August 16, 1985 – her twenty-seventh birthday – was squeezed into downtime between performing at Live Aid and starting work on her third album.

The Live Aid slot – three songs, middle of the bill, at Philadelphia's JFK Stadium – makes fascinating viewing now. She dances onto the stage and immediately shouts: "Come on, people, put your hands together!" There are 90,000 people in the stadium, and she's taking command like a veteran rock star. "I can't hear you!" she goads. "How about you people at the back?" The 45,000 or so at the back roar approval.

That said, she was used to large concert crowds, having just finished her first headlining tour. It was a sold-out, 40-date jaunt across America and Canada, playing to arenas of hyped-up young girls. She came out of it aware of how much power she wielded; reviewer Mary Edgar Smith of the *Atlanta Journal-Constitution* got it right when she commented dryly: "She will be a force to be reckoned with."

Previous Pages: Contemplating her reflection in March 1985, the month 'Material Girl' hit Number 2 on the US *Billboard* chart.

Right: Madonna's look was instantly recognizable and easy to copy, so stocking lycra minis and studded belts became one of the key styles of the mid-1980s.

CHAPTER 4
TRUE BLUE

Released as she ascended to rule-breaking superstardom – it sold 25 million copies – True Blue established Madonna as a pop songwriter of note, and one who sparked cultural debate with singles such as 'Papa Don't Preach'.

Madonna at a press conference for *Shanghai Surprise*, in which she co-starred with Sean Penn.

TRUE BLUE

Madonna consolidates her fame with the blockbuster True Blue, *selling 25 million copies and becoming the most successful (and controversial) female singer of the 1980s. She also marries Sean Penn and acts alongside him in* Shanghai Surprise, *a spectacular flop.*

Second albums, according to rock myth, are traditionally "difficult". *Like a Virgin* had been anything but. As 1985 ended, it had shipped six million copies, and won the Top Pop Album trophy at the Billboard Music Awards (one of seven gongs Madonna took home that night). No pressure, then, for her third album, *Live to Tell* (or *True Blue*, as it was soon retitled).

Following up the record that had made her a cultural figure was, in fact, only moderately stressful. Working with old friend Steve Bray and Patrick Leonard, her third producer in as many albums, she was now in a position to see her ideas fully realized. Co-writing and -producing every track, she was able to explore and stretch herself. This time, she and Leonard factored in more complex sounds, along with the usual dance-pop. While still foregrounding grooves and beats, *True Blue's* nine tracks were more sophisticated than anything she'd done hitherto. Flamenco guitar, classical music and an early bit of sampling (in this case, snatches of dialogue from the James Cagney film *White Heat*) found their way in, and she was also confident enough to slip in a big, soft-rock ballad. 'Live to Tell', with its very 80s guitar and slow, contemplative vocal, is one of the most enduring power ballads of a decade that produced more than its share (Berlin's 'Take My Breath Away' and Bette Midler's 'Wind Beneath My Wings' being just two of them).

And she was braver with her voice. Lacking range and richness, it had always been the area where producers had had to work to bring out its best. Siedah Garrett, a backing vocalist on *True Blue*, told me when I interviewed her in the 1980s, "Madonna can't sing – but she's a singer." It was meant as a compliment: Garrett's own voice had the heft and power Madonna's didn't, but Madonna was proof that vocal technique needn't be the deciding factor in a singer's career.

In fact, her girlish voice had its own strengths. There was always plenty of raw emotion in it, along with a sweetness that worked winningly with her disco anthems. As with that other deceptively weak singer Kylie Minogue, it wasn't the voice but what she did with it – and few dance-pop vocalists have been able to convey joy and pain as genuinely. On *True Blue*, she went for some big vocal moments, such as 'Live to Tell', 'Open Your Heart' and 'Love Makes the World Go Round'.

Varied as it was, it was also cohesive. Kicking off with 'Papa Don't Preach', an immediate stone-cold classic, it veered from ballad to rock to dance, all distinctly different but all strong, sleek and shot through with emotion. This was the record where she found her feet as a lyricist, layering tunes with personal references. 'Jimmy Jimmy' was inspired by her childhood crush on James Dean; 'La Isla Bonita' by her passion for Hispanic culture (which had already been referenced in the 'Borderline' video).

Left: A pensive Madonna on the set of the 'Papa Don't Preach' video, Staten Island, May 1986.

Left: A dyed-blonde Madonna at
the American Music Awards, 1987,
where she won Favourite Pop/Rock
Female Video Artist.

"This album is dedicated to my husband, the coolest guy in the universe."

Madonna

The title track, meanwhile, was a love song to Sean Penn, who got one of the "special thanx" in the credits: "This album is dedicated to my husband, the coolest guy in the universe." Her infatuation with Penn makes itself felt throughout the album – her singing is buoyant and effortless.

It was, you could say, the first record that had her stamp all over it. Even 'Papa Don't Preach' was manifestly a "Madonna song", though it's the song that is least "hers"; composer Brian Elliot was responsible for most of the lyric. Its teen-pregnancy theme was so provocative that battles lines were immediately drawn, and for the first time in her career, Madonna was supported by Tipper Gore's PMRC organization, who called the track "an important song, and a good one" because of the main character's decision to keep her unborn baby.

Family-planning advocates were incensed, their views encapsulated in a demand by high-profile lawyer Gloria Allred that Madonna record another song that reflected the pro-choice view. The *New York Times* reported in August 1986 that the director of Planned Parenthood of New York City had called on Warner Bros to donate 25 per cent of the song's profits to organizations that promoted "responsible sexual behaviour". Madonna herself, after initially telling the *Times* that she expected the song to be misinterpreted, refused to be drawn into the debate.

When released as a single, in June 1986, 'Papa Don't Preach' hit Number 1, shipping 500,000 copies in the US, a testament to its brilliance as a song, as well as to the controversy. Though Madonna was a 27-year-old pretending to be a teenager in the song, it was one of the most heartfelt vocals on the record. The lyric mirrored aspects of her own life: she was a Catholic girl who had a complicated relationship with her father, questioning his views while also seeking his guidance. Presumably, she didn't get pregnant and consider marrying her boyfriend, but that was a moot point. Her delivery rang so true that, at some level, she had obviously lived the song.

Everything about the album, from the cover shot by Herb Ritts to the music itself, marked her ascent to the top echelon of pop stardom. Ritts photographed her with her head thrown back and neck exposed, as if she were sculpted in marble. Chosen from 60 rolls of film shot by Ritts, the image, printed in shades of grey and blue, made her look less pop queen than old-time movie star. In North America, the image was considered strong enough to sell the album without her name or the title on it; in Europe, the label played safe and printed them on the sleeve.

It was profoundly different from the two previous LP sleeves, which had portrayed her as first a confrontational pop chick, then a boy toy. *True Blue*'s cover was made with posterity in mind. It was both of its moment and classic; 28 years later, it's still arresting.

The pared-down new look was also the first significant image makeover of her career. With the *True Blue* sleeve, Madonna bade farewell to her punky, bag-lady self and went for heavy glamour. "If you spend a couple of years wearing lots of layers of clothes and jewelry," she explained to Michael Gross, "you get the urge to take it all off just for relief." This streamlined, pristine version of Madonna was a statement of intent. The ingénue no longer, she was literally ready for her close-up.

Taking off her "layers" distanced her a little from both her teen fanbase and contemporaries like Boy George, whose jumble-sale quirkiness was starting to look dated by contrast. George, predictably, was having none of it. In a mid-80s TV interview, he responded waspishly to the suggestion that he was "last year's thing, visually". He snapped at the interviewer: "At the risk of sounding conceited, there would have been no Madonna... without Culture Club." And, in fact, his claim is not entirely without merit: the two did meet on one of Madonna's early trips to London, and she may well have made some mental notes about his appearance. There was certainly some visual overlap between his New Romantic finery and her Second Hand Rose style, but it was probably his fearlessness that impressed her most. His insistence on being himself – creating a new identity through dressing up – would have resonated with a fellow Catholic who had left home, dropped her surname and become "Madonna".

There was a rather sad footnote to her stylistic reinvention. Maripol, co-architect of the bangles-and-crucifixes look, went bankrupt in 1986. Her fashion business had initially thrived thanks to the style Madonna made famous, but once the singer became a superstar, dozens of other designers rushed out cheap copies. She couldn't compete on production costs, and went out of business. "How can you survive when millions of people start making their most horrible, supposedly rubber jewellery which was actually made out of plastic?" she told MadonnaTribe.com.

True Blue was released in June 1986. In America, its first single, 'Live to Tell', had come out three months previously and hit Number 1, neatly setting up the album for a big, splashy success. It duly went to Number 1, staying there for five weeks (and six in Britain).

Critics were respectful. She was now too big to dismiss: you had only to walk down the street to see her effect on fashion – even the haute couture of Karl Lagerfeld and Christian Lacroix showed her influence – while newsstands were stuffed with interviews and articles examining the Madonna phenomenon.

Furthermore, she had served her apprenticeship, musically speaking. She'd done her time with big-name producers, learning the ropes and acquiring proper skills. Thus, *Rolling Stone* reviewer Davitt Sigerson wrote: *"True Blue* may generate fewer sales... than *Like a Virgin*, but it sets her up as an artist for the long run." (In fact, it became her most successful album, selling around 25 million copies to *Like a Virgin*'s 21 million.) And while it wasn't "revolutionary", according to the *Los Angeles Times'* Robert Hilburn, it was "imaginative, highly energized pop".

Sigerson and Hilburn's views were tempered with a good-but-not-great cautiousness that was typical of 80s reviewers. *True Blue* (and the first two albums) comes off far better in modern-day reappraisals. Sal Cinquemani of the online magazine *Slant* acknowledged that, with this record, she "made the transition from pop tart to consummate artist", while SputnikMusic.com's Frederick Metzengerstein said: "Chock full of catchy hooks, twerk-worthy choruses and upbeat, inspired songwriting."

Twerk-worthy? And yet, why not? There's something apt about linking a Madonna album to twerking, a subject that spawned enormous coverage in 2013. It's also not unreasonable to suggest that, if Madonna hadn't existed, the most famous exponent of twerking, Miley Cyrus, wouldn't have found herself at the MTV Awards in August 2013, touching her crotch with a giant foam hand and thrusting her backside at Robin Thicke.

The fact that Cyrus's generation grew up feeling comfortable with exuberant displays of female sexual assertiveness can be traced

Above: Video was an intrinsic part of Madonna's success. She received the Video Vanguard trophy at the 1986 MTV Awards.

Right: In Philadelphia on 1987's Who's That Girl Tour. The Pope urged young Italians to boycott the tour.

straight back to Madonna. In fact, Cyrus acknowledged her debt in February 2014, when she invited Madonna to perform with her on an *MTV Unplugged* special; tellingly, when Madonna sauntered onstage from the back of the auditorium, the crowd squealed far more loudly than it had for Cyrus.

True Blue produced five singles, three of which ('Live to Tell', 'Papa Don't Preach' and 'Open Your Heart') got to Number 1. The others – the title track and 'La Isla Bonita' – reached Numbers 3 and 4, respectively. They came out between March 1986 and February 1987, a new one popping out every couple of months, imprinting her indelibly into the cultural mainstream. It was an incredible release rate, and all the more so because she was involved in most aspects, such as choosing photos and approving artwork. Each had to be accompanied by a video, amounting to a work schedule with almost no breaks. What time she had away from promoting the records was spent on projects with Sean Penn – together, they made the movie *Shanghai Surprise* and did a three-night workshop production of the David Rabe play *Goose and Tomtom*.

Just contemplating her 1986 activities induces exhaustion. Singles were followed by videos, which were followed by red-carpet appearances (at the premieres of Penn's new film *At Close Range*, and their joint film *Shanghai Surprise*), which were followed by the first filming for her own new movie, *Who's That Girl*. And on and on: endless promotion and new projects and charity appearances (AIDS research was her chosen cause). It reads like the schedule of someone whose career was her lifeblood, demanding great sacrifices in her personal life. But perhaps they didn't feel like sacrifices, because every hit (at the end of 1986, her career tally was 11 Top 10 singles and three Top 10 LPs) brought her closer to her goal of "ruling the world". When she'd said it on *American Bandstand* three years before, many had scoffed, but now it didn't seem quite so implausible.

Her only misstep in 1986 was *Shanghai Surprise*, a film allegedly so bad that it has since acquired almost legendary status. She played a missionary and Penn a fortune hunter, who join forces in 1937 China to find a consignment of opium she needed for her patients. Unsurprisingly, they fall in love, and run up against an assortment of villains who also want the opium. George Harrison, who co-

produced through his Handmade Films company, had a cameo as a nightclub owner.

On paper, it must have looked like movie dynamite. Madonna had only just had a hit with *Desperately Seeking Susan*, and was still wafting along in the glow of positive reviews, so pairing her with a fast-rising young actor would surely have people buying tickets just to see their on-screen chemistry. That they were married to each other was a PR bonus. (Madonna's photo was much larger than Penn's on one of the cinema posters, suggesting the producers knew who the real draw was.) The plot was full of scrapes, explosions and car chases, and Madonna revealed unexpected action-heroine chops when she kicked a villain where it hurt. The Hong Kong set looked great. To top it off, an ex-Beatle was involved. It seemed like the closest thing the film business had to a safe bet.

The bad reviews felt like an onslaught. It was as if critics had been waiting for the chance to lay into her (and, by extension, Penn): having had the audacity to decide she could make movies, she was going to pay in the form of some of the worst reviews she'd ever had. Penn, as the more experienced actor, came in for a drubbing that blamed him for getting involved.

The plot itself was gleefully picked apart, with the American box-office bible *Variety* deeming the lead characters' relationship "completely illogical", while Madonna's guileless missionary "makes no sense at all". Sheila Benson of the *Los Angeles Times* noted the "absolute obtuseness of the screenplay", which was based on the improbable idea that a lone missionary would take it upon herself to find missing opium in a huge, unfamiliar city.

The dialogue also incited derision while other reviewers poured scorn on the portrayal of Shanghai as a city packed with inscrutable Oriental clichés, including a sexpot called China Doll. In the trailer, the place was described as "a place of mystery", thus combining stereotypes with Western condescension.

Meanwhile, the acting was roundly panned. Madonna was "wimpy" and Penn "stiff", said the *San Francisco Chronicle*'s Peter

Right: One of the seven costumes worn during the Who's That Girl Tour. Her famous black basque is just visible.

Top and Left: Her talent for reinvention is evident in this 1987 shot: she's come a long way from the punky scruff look.

Above: Now a global star, Madonna makes her way through the paparazzi, escorted by bodyguards.

Stack; reappraising it in 2007, *Edge Boston*'s Phil Hall claimed they were miscast and "charisma-challenged". Madonna, in his view, was simply "incompetent".

The fundamental mistake had been to assume that the couple could carry a film on their relationship and star-power alone. But Penn wasn't a comedy actor, while Madonna's previous experience had been in a film that basically let her play herself. Going against type as a missionary – and a missionary who was too gorgeous to be believable – she floundered. The script was full of lines inspired by 30s screwball comedies but these sounded wrong coming from her, no matter how earnestly delivered. The deficiencies of the plot did the rest, and *Shanghai Surprise* ended up recouping only $2.3 million of its $17 million budget.

Film history doesn't teem with real-life couples who also had screen chemistry (among the few that did were Nicolas Cage and Patricia Arquette, Elizabeth Taylor and Richard Burton, and Meg Ryan and Dennis Quaid), but it would be years before any other pair would attract such opprobrium: Jennifer Lopez and Ben Affleck for *Gigli* in 2003. Madonna may have taken some comfort in knowing she wasn't the only pop star/ actress to have been savaged by the press.

Shanghai Surprise received five Golden Raspberry nominations, including Worst Picture, Worst Actress and Worst Original Song (for the title track, sung by George Harrison and embellished with Eastern motifs such as gongs). Madonna "won" for Worst Actress (and would receive another Razzie in 1987 for *Who's That Girl*, plus three more after that for other pictures).

But *Shanghai Surprise* was a blip in an otherwise stormingly successful year, which was capped by *True Blue* becoming the world's best-selling album of 1986. She took home a mantelpiece-ful of trophies for it: Favorite Pop/Rock Female at the American Music Awards, three Billboard Music awards, the MTV Video Vanguard statuette and Favorite Female Musical Performer at the People's Choice ceremony. She was even Sexiest Female Artist, according to the readers of *Rolling Stone*, who also voted her Best Female Singer.

As betokened by the Video Vanguard citation, she was as much a visual creation as a musical one. In fact, in the popular imagination, the product she was selling – her music – was starting to be regarded as something to listen to while watching her onscreen. She was quite aware of this: at the end of 1984, she had released a compilation of four of her videos, and saw it sell two million copies. It was the biggest-selling "music videocassette" (as the industry called them) of 1985, proving her mastery of the still relatively new medium.

It's safe to say that, had there been no imagery to cause a furore, tracks like 'Open Your Heart' and the 1989 single 'Like a Prayer' would have passed nearly unnoticed. 'Open Your Heart' is a particularly good example. Lyrically speaking, it was actually one of her more innocuous numbers, but in conjunction with its video, it became another piece of evidence – as far as parents were concerned – that she was on a mission to corrupt American youth. But more of that in a moment.

In the most basic sense, Madonna's videos gave her singles extra oomph, by showing her singing and dancing while looking impossibly beautiful. But they could also be symbolism-laden works of art. For every straightforward clip (say, 'Live to Tell', a meat-and-potatoes montage of scenes from the film *At Close Range*, in which it featured), there was one that was thought-provoking and cinematic.

'Papa Don't Preach', for example, was more film than pop video. Directed by James Foley and filmed in Staten Island, it featured waterfront scenes and glimpses of working-class neighbourhoods that echoed *Saturday Night Fever*, which had been made just across the river in Brooklyn. Madonna could have been a character from that film. Playing an Italian homegirl with issues – namely, an unplanned pregnancy with a boy who was every father's nightmare – she was almost the female version of *Saturday Night Fever*'s Tony Manero.

The acting, with character actor Danny Aiello playing Papa, was instinctive and graceful. Clearly, Madonna *could* play a character other than herself; every gesture was believable. The most compelling scenes were those in which she revealed her pregnancy to the two most important people in her life, her father and her garage-mechanic boyfriend, played by Alex McArthur. Looking waifish and anxious, she awaited their reactions, and was assured that both would stand by her. Again mimicking *Saturday Night Fever*, it ends with two characters embracing as they take tentative steps toward an uncertain new life.

On a deeper level, it provoked questions about who makes the decisions in a woman's life – herself, or her family and boyfriend? Reflecting on it in 2009, Madonna defended it as a show of female strength. Much of her need to shock and awe was generated by wanting to defy the patriarchy – especially her father, the quintessential Italian-American patriarch. It was nominated for three MTV Awards, and won the Best Female category.

The video for 'Open Your Heart' (the album's fourth single, and fifth Number 1 of her career) was another small masterpiece. Sean Penn was originally pencilled in as director, but fashion photographer Jean-Baptiste Mondino ended up with the job. (How would it have turned out in Penn's hands? It's hard to imagine him coming up with anything as seedily glamorous, and distinctly European, as Mondino's effort). Madonna played a peep-show dancer, performing in a black-satin bustier for a group of men and women whose reactions ranged from boggle-eyed lust to embarrassed aloofness.

Felix Howard (later a vice president at EMI Music Publishing, then a child model and actor) played a little boy who managed to sneak past the doorman at Madonna's workplace. Once inside, he stared in shock at a poster of her in the club foyer. Catching her eye by moonwalking – which she rewarded with a borderline-saucy kiss on the lips – he enticed her to leave her job. Suddenly, magically, the two were standing outside the strip joint, preparing to make their

getaway. Then they literally danced off into the sunset, the little kid and the go-go dancer.

As with 'Papa Don't Preach', it was compelling. Mondino turned it into a story of innocence versus corruption, bathing Felix Howard in golden light and the adult men in sleazy greens and blues. As Madonna danced, he shot from behind, showing slack-jawed customers through her open legs. At least one was a woman, and there was a gay male couple, a nod to Madonna's pan-gender, pan-sexual appeal.

MTV was initially unsure about whether to show it, and, sure enough, its depiction of the little boy in the strip club provoked complaints. Some critics, however, saw it as a bit of fun, with Bruce Handy of *Vogue* praising it as "a witty take on female sexuality held prisoner by neurotic male desire". Its meaning has been debated down the years: was Madonna actually a prisoner in the strip club, or a free spirit still capable of dancing down the street, unscathed by her experience? Feminist academic Susan Bordo wrote, "I would say that, ultimately, this video is entirely about Madonna's body, the narrative context virtually irrelevant."

And yet... taken on its own, without the video, the song would have engendered no controversy whatever. Musically and lyrically, it was a typical Madonna love ditty, in which she pleaded with the inattentive object of her affections to notice her. The lyric promised/

"True Blue *may generate fewer sales... than* Like a Virgin, *but it sets her up as an artist for the long run.*"

Davitt Sigerson

warned that there was no escaping her, because she could run as fast as he could (something that seemed entirely likely, as she had been working out and her physique was now noticeably more muscular). Heard now, it has a stalkerish undertow, perhaps, but this is essentially as conventional as pop songs get. It was the video that made it into something more.

For what it's worth, 'Open Your Heart' was voted one of the 50 Sexiest Video Moments of all time on the music channel VH1, which suggested that many viewers weren't very bothered about the artistry or the message, because... well... it was Madonna in a basque, doing acrobatic things with her lower body. Her physical flexibility was also acknowledged by an MTV Awards nomination for Best Choreography in a Video (in fairness, young Howard's moonwalking probably also contributed). It was nominated in two other categories, including Best Female, where she lost to herself (for 'Papa Don't Preach').

True Blue's final single, 'La Isla Bonita', was another track that was controversial only because of its video. The song itself was a flamenco-accented travelogue about the mythical Spanish island of San Pedro and the boy she met there; it yearningly recalled carefree times with the welcoming, beautiful natives, and she sang the last verse in Spanish to emphasize her attachment to both island and boy. She even wore a gaucho hat in the cover photo.

Though Madonna probably wouldn't record such a song today – its portrayal of Hispanic culture as indolent raised some eyebrows even in 1986 – its charm is undeniable. "A perfectly conceived pop record," said David Browne of *Entertainment Weekly*, and it's still loved by fans today. Apparently, the song was first offered to Michael Jackson, but it's impossible to imagine him doing a better job with it.

The video, though, was the real talking point. "San Pedro" (actually a Hispanic neighbourhood in Los Angeles) was a place of Spanglish cliché. Madonna wore a flamenco dress, the whitewashed buildings were crumbling and there was a working-age male who evidently had nothing more pressing to do in the middle of the day than play guitar on a sofa in the street. The entire neighbourhood, in fact, was shown languidly dancing in the street. When Madonna swished down the stairs in her red dress, it turned into a mini-fiesta, with everyone smiling and dancing. At the end, she danced down the street, presumably back to her own life as the party continued behind her.

"Even though she lives [in the barrio], her reality is clearly separated from that of the Latinos," wrote Santiago Fouz-Hernandez, while the blogger JBNYC took her to task on the website MadonnaTribe.com. "Perhaps less justifiable is Madonna's appropriation of world cultures... she took on the Latin culture to stylize her La Isla Bonita video". The blogger compared it to her championing of LGBT culture, which worked to gay people's advantage because it gave Middle America a window onto their culture that hadn't existed before. (In this way, Madonna also paid her debt to the gay men who were her first fans, back in her Paradise Garage and Danceteria days. Interestingly, Madonna's modern-day Mini-Me, Lady Gaga, is highly vocal in her support of LGBT people, causing some to complain that she has taken up their cause uninvited and that her intervention is unappreciated.)

But while seeing Madonna's empathy with gay men in a positive light, JBNYC was less convinced by her forays into ethnic empathy. Her borrowing of Latin (and later Indian and Japanese) styles for videos and photo shoots lacked substance, amounting to mere decoration. Nonetheless, the song is still a much-loved part of her catalogue, and has the power to galvanize crowds when she plays it live. Reviewing the opening UK date of her 2008 Sticky & Sweet Tour, the *Daily Telegraph*'s Isabel Albiston noted that although the audience was visibly unmoved by her new songs, "the energy picked up during 'La Isla Bonita', when she skipped around the stage [with] a procession of violin players".

'La Isla Bonita', along with the rest of *True Blue* (except the tracks 'Jimmy Jimmy' and 'Love Makes the World Go Round'), featured on her first international tour, in 1987. The 37-date jaunt was called the Who's That Girl World Tour, to publicize the next thing on her agenda, a film and soundtrack LP of that name. Though it sold out because of the success of *True Blue*, that album was in effect behind her. The Who's That Girl Tour was both a farewell to the past and a step into the future. She played to vast audiences that summer – 130,000 at one gig in Paris alone. It was the start of her imperial phase.

Left: The famous bustier, seen here in Minnesota in 1988, fetched $72,000 at auction in 2011.

Previous Pages: Expressing herself: a striking onstage close-up in Rotterdam, July 1990.

Right: Though there were multiple costume changes during the show, the corset became the most iconic piece.

Thirty is a watershed age for a pop star, and so it proved for Madonna and her 1958 superstar cohort, which included Price and Michael Jackson. All three were born within three months of each other, in the same sector of the Midwest, and all found themselves at artistic reckoning points during the summer of 1988. Prince began to delve into spirituality with *Lovesexy* (and duly lost sales), while Jackson was becoming increasingly sensitized to the plight of the world (his efforts to change things would surface as his next album, *Dangerous*).

Madonna also felt the need to take stock. At 30, she was one of the most famous women in the world, commanding a following so large that even offshoot releases, such as the 1988 video album *Ciao Italia: Live from Italy* (a film souvenir of a gig in Turin on the Who's That Girl Tour), sold hundreds of thousands of copies. But she also had a faltering marriage, which she blamed on the couple's "high-visibility life". The splintering of her relationship was deeply painful; in 1991, she would reveal to Lynn Hirschberg of *Vanity Fair* how much she continued to miss her ex-husband. "I still go to see his movies. I have to see his movies, because sometimes that's the only way I can see him." (She was several boyfriends down the line by then, but clearly Penn still exerted an influence.) And as her marriage was crumbling, she was also dismayed by the response to her acting ventures.

Thus, by the time she started the sessions for *Like a Prayer*, she had plenty to write about. Recording began in September 1988 and the songs poured out. Their titles were her most sombre yet – there was no 'Holiday' or 'La Isla Bonita', nothing to assure the listener that the tune they were about to hear was a hands-in-the-air stormer. Instead, the track listing was redolent of hard times and soldiering on. One song, 'Till Death Do Us Part', directly addressed her domestic problems, while there was also a meditative ballad about her mother's death ('Promise to Try') and another describing her fractured childhood relationship with her father ('Oh Father'). The title track addressed God, portraying Him almost as a lover – the lyric could very much be taken either way – while 'Pray for Spanish Eyes' tackled AIDS. 'Keep it Together' could be heard as a call for worldwide unity, or as something urgent and personal, and the album's final track had the starkest possible title: 'Act of Contrition'. (Which turned out to be deceptive – 'Act of Contrition' is the LP's wildcard, an improvised

goof-up featuring Prince on guitar and a backwards-running tape, the whole thing culminating in Madonna snarling about restaurant reservations. So she hadn't entirely lost her sense of humour.)

As with her previous albums, this one was recorded quickly – just six months from the start of the sessions to the finished item hitting the shops. For a sense of how efficiently she worked, consider that many of the key tracks – including 'Promise to Try', 'Till Death Do Us Part' and the title track – were written in a single fortnight at the start of 1989. Collaborating with Pat Leonard and Steve Bray again, she would turn up in the studio with a notebook and write lyrics on the spot. During the writing sessions, Leonard was also busy producing another album, so Madonna worked around his schedule, coming in on Saturdays or whenever he had a weekday off. Industriously composing, she took no more than four hours per song to transform fragments of ideas into workable lyrics. As Bray revealed to Chris Heath of *Smash Hits*, "She writes in a stream of mood, really. I'm sure [the album] was a kind of cathartic thing to do."

Half a dozen numbers ended up not used, including 'Supernatural', 'Love Attack' and 'Just a Dream'. They didn't chime with the overall reflective tone, which seems rather a shame, because the way Leonard tells it, 'Supernatural', at least, was pretty nifty. "It's about sleeping with a ghost. It's a real kind of weird funk tune with a very strange groove." The other lost tracks have had varying fates. 'Just a Dream' was later

recorded by Madonna's backing singer Marilyn Martin (with Madonna on backing vocals), but it failed to make a splash, while 'First is a Kiss' – described by Bray as a "safe sex song" – regularly surfaces online.

(It's common practice for at least some artists to allow unused material to be recorded by others; one of the most successful of these transfers was Nick Kamen's cover of 'Each Time You Break My Heart', a discarded track from the *True Blue* sessions. It became a Number 5 British hit, and model-turned-singer Kamen struck up enough of a friendship to persuade Pat Leonard to produce his second album and Madonna herself to sing on it. Lush-lipped and smouldering as he was, however, Kamen was no pop star, and today is mainly remembered for a 1985 TV ad for Levi's, in which he stripped off his jeans in a laundrette.)

Once recording was completed, Madonna reconvened with Herb Ritts, the photographer for *True Blue*, to shoot the cover. The picture chosen further reinforced the idea that this record was different from the others. For one thing, it was the first to be in full colour, and the first not to show her face – instead, Ritts photographed her at waist-level, focusing on her hands, which were resting on the rolled-down waistband of her jeans. But the central point of the shot was the ornate, Indian-style necklace dangling down from her neck, and a starburst "Madonna" logo, topped by a little crown.

It was sexually confrontational, in the sense that her focus was her

"She writes in a stream of mood, really. I'm sure [the album] was a kind of cathartic thing to do."

Steve Bray

crotch, and her hands were seemingly in the process of removing her jeans. It was almost a female answer to the Rolling Stones' aggressively masculine *Sticky Fingers* sleeve – yet there was a distinctly non-sexual feel. Rather, the hands and jeans and necklace conveyed warmth and an earthy spirituality. The necklace, and nine gold Indian rings on her fingers, drew attention from those half-removed jeans and gave the shot an exoticism that, at the very least, announced that this was a different sort of Madonna album. The packaging was even impregnated with patchouli oil, to mimic church incense. It was a classic Madonna sleight-of-hand – by simply using her magpie approach to other cultures (in this case, by wearing Asian jewellery), she directed the public's attention away from Madonna the Sexbomb toward Madonna the Artist.

Warner Bros put out word that *Like a Prayer* bore little resemblance to its predecessors. "We think it's going to be a significant album," said the label's head of press, Bob Merlis, to Bruce Britt of the *Los Angeles Daily News*. "Sure, it's deep stuff, but it's not obscure or gratuitously arty." Steve Bray said more or less the same thing, warning fans not to expect an uptempo dance album.

It wasn't that there was nothing boogie-able about *Like a Prayer*. The soulful self-empowerment jam 'Express Yourself' was as catchy as anything she'd done, and so was the title track, which incorporated her first experiment with gospel. There was the breezy little pop ditty 'Cherish' – try to resist wriggling around to that on the dance

floor – and even the 60s-style frothiness of 'Dear Jessie' lent itself to dancing. But, as Bray implied, it was the first record she'd made in which lyrics and sonic experimentation were prioritized over beats. It was as much statement as album: she was asking – demanding – to be taken seriously.

The album was slated for release on March 21, 1989, and its first single – the title track – two weeks before that, on March 7. But the American public got its inaugural taste of the new music on March 2, in a Pepsi commercial. She had signed a deal, reportedly for $5 million, to endorse the soft drink, so Pepsi got first dibs on the single. This was an early example of cross-promotion: Pepsi received the right to broadcast the single before it was officially released, and also agreed to sponsor her next tour; in return for lending her image and music, Madonna got incalculable exposure in the ads, which could only help sales of the new album.

The ad, directed by Joe Pytka (who had also overseen Michael Jackson's Pepsi commercials), was a model of spirited inclusiveness. Over a two-minute excerpt from the track, there were scenes of Madonna as both a child and an adult – in a Catholic school, then singing with a group

---

Above Left: Next stop Versailles: performing 'Vogue' at the MTV Awards, Los Angeles, September 1990.

Above Right: Dressed as Breathless Mahoney in the "Dick Tracy" segment of the Blond Ambition Tour.

of teenagers and then a gospel choir, the entire cast surging toward a joyous finale. There was even a glimpse, at the end, of her raising a can of Pepsi. It was youthful, upbeat, and true enough to her personality not to feel like a sell-out. (Explaining her decision to do the ad, Madonna said that she'd been intrigued by the challenge of producing a commercial that was both artistic and popular.)

Pepsi aired a teaser ad a couple of weeks beforehand to let the public know the commercial was on its way. Anyone who assumes that the hyping-up of media events is a modern phenomenon should see the Pepsi teaser. "No matter where you are in the world on March 2," it demanded, "get to a TV and see Pepsi present Madonna." Essentially, a TV commercial was being pitched as a major cultural event – and maybe it was. Madonna, after all, was globally famous – she was frequently called "the most famous woman in the world", which probably wasn't far off the mark – and this was the debut of her first new music since 1986.

At any rate. around 250 million people in 40 countries watched the commercial, which in America aired during the top-rated sitcom *The Cosby Show*. In 1996, Nancy J. Vickers was oddly prescient when she described the Madonna/Pepsi tie-in as "a hymn to the global capabilities of the age of electronic reproduction". (These same capabilities would be recognized by Madonna herself as the digital age progressed; in 2000, she would be in the vanguard of artists who used the internet to broadcast live gigs, when she played a show at London's Brixton Academy. There were 4,500 people in the actual building, and around 9 million online.)

The ad would undoubtedly have been remembered merely as an effective corporate/artistic hook-up if the official video for 'Like a Prayer' hadn't debuted on MTV the next day. The storm caused by it eclipsed all previous Madonna controversies, causing Pepsi to sever its links with her and, according to wilder reports, the Pope himself to demand the video be banned from Italian television.

The video, directed by long-time associate Mary Lambert, was a mini-drama that had the singer witnessing an attack on a young woman, and fleeing to a nearby church for safety. There, surrounded by burning candles and effigies of saints, she encountered an effigy of a black saint, which came to life and kissed her. He was then wrongly

arrested for attacking the woman, but was freed from prison after Madonna intervened. Burning crosses and stigmata heightened the tension. In the last scene, the couple rejoiced by singing with a gospel choir while the song played out.

MTV itself had dubbed 'Like a Prayer' "Madonna's most controversial video", and so it proved. Condemnation was immediate, most of it sparked by the interracial dalliance between Madonna and the saint. Religious groups, led by the Mississippi-based American Family Association and the bishop of Corpus Christi, Texas, the Most Reverend René Gracida, found it blasphemous and called for a boycott of Pepsi products. Though Pepsi had had nothing to do with the video – the company hadn't even seen it before it premiered on March 3 – it became the target of complaints that should have been directed at MTV, the channel that had aired it. Some angry viewers even assumed that the video was the Pepsi ad, which must have required a leap of imagination: mainstream brands like Pepsi were hardly in the business of making commercials laden with provocative religious imagery. "It's an unfortunate situation," company spokesman Tod MacKenzie acknowledged to the Associated Press.

Left: Singing 'Like a Virgin' on tour in 1990. Note Madonna's hair extensions, which often got tangled in her headset.

Above: Flexing her muscles at one of three sold-out shows at London's Wembley Stadium in 1990.

Left: She switched from long hair
extensions to this curly do when
the extensions damaged her hair.

Overleaf: Singing on a bed – choreographer
Vincent Paterson said the aim of the tour
was to "break every rule we can".

Others were less troubled by the "blasphemy" than by the flaming crosses. "It is the symbol of the Ku Klux Klan's reign of terror," wrote Phil Kloer of the Cox News Service. "It exploits a symbol of evil to sell records."

A few, however, saw the video as Madonna and Lambert had intended – as a story of right and wrong. "It was about overcoming racism... overcoming the fear of telling the truth," Madonna explained on Australian TV at the height of the furore. Her intention, she said, was to encourage people who were "afraid to... stand up for someone else."

One of the most robust defences of 'Like a Prayer' was mounted by a clergyman. The Rev. Andrew M. Greeley in the magazine *America: The National Catholic Review*. "This is blasphemy?" he questioned contemptuously. "Only for the prurient... who come to the video determined to read their own twisted sexual hang-ups into it."

Nonetheless, protestors kept up pressure on Pepsi to drop Madonna, and, a month later, it did. In the end, the commercial was shown only twice on American TV (though it continued to run in other countries). She was said to have been allowed to keep her $5 million fee, and the company has continued to use pop stars in its ads (including, most recently, One Direction).

The outcome was deemed a victory for the religious right, which increasingly had been using the threat of consumer boycotts to register its disapproval about the content of certain TV shows. Liberty groups were concerned about the ramifications of major brands succumbing to this kind of moral pressure – and there was also the simple wrongheadedness of Pepsi being held to account for a video it had nothing to do with. "It raises disturbing questions about the intelligence of the American people," said advertising expert Bob Garfield in the *Philadelphia Inquirer*. "Can't they register the difference between an ad with Madonna and a music video with Madonna?"

Madonna herself later said, "I couldn't believe how out-of-control the whole Pepsi thing got." But it did album sales no harm: *Like a Prayer* came out two weeks later, reached the Number 1 slot a couple of weeks after that and, within two months, had been certified double platinum. It eventually sold 15 million copies.

"I couldn't believe how out-of-control the whole Pepsi thing got."
Madonna

More importantly, perhaps, it validated her as a musician, attracting the best reviews she'd had to date. The album was analyzed at length across the media, and the consensus was that she had finally produced a work of true artistic merit. Even Robert Christgau, not always a fan, admitted it was "challenging, thrilling". The *Austin American-Statesman*'s Kevin Philly, meanwhile, simply had a question: "So when did Madonna find the time to make an album as good as *Like A Prayer*?"

That sentiment was echoed decades later, when the album was re-released in digitally remastered form and many publications reviewed it again. One of the only holdouts was the venerable New York punk fanzine *Trouser Press*, which reappraised it in 2008 and pronounced it "flawless and hollow... pretentious ...would be stronger if her voice bore even a trace of conviction". Pretentious? Hollow? Surely this was unjustified? Well, "pretentious" could technically hold water. She'd travelled from the froth of 'Holiday' and Boy Toys to a completely new persona that demanded to be viewed differently, and inevitably some would think it rang false. In the eyes of non-believers, once a Boy Toy, always a Boy Toy, so in that light, *Like a Prayer* must indeed have seemed "pretentious".

But hollow? Lacking conviction? That's harder to comprehend. One thing Madonna could never be accused of, then or now, is insincerity. If *Trouser Press*'s reviewers failed to detect real emotion

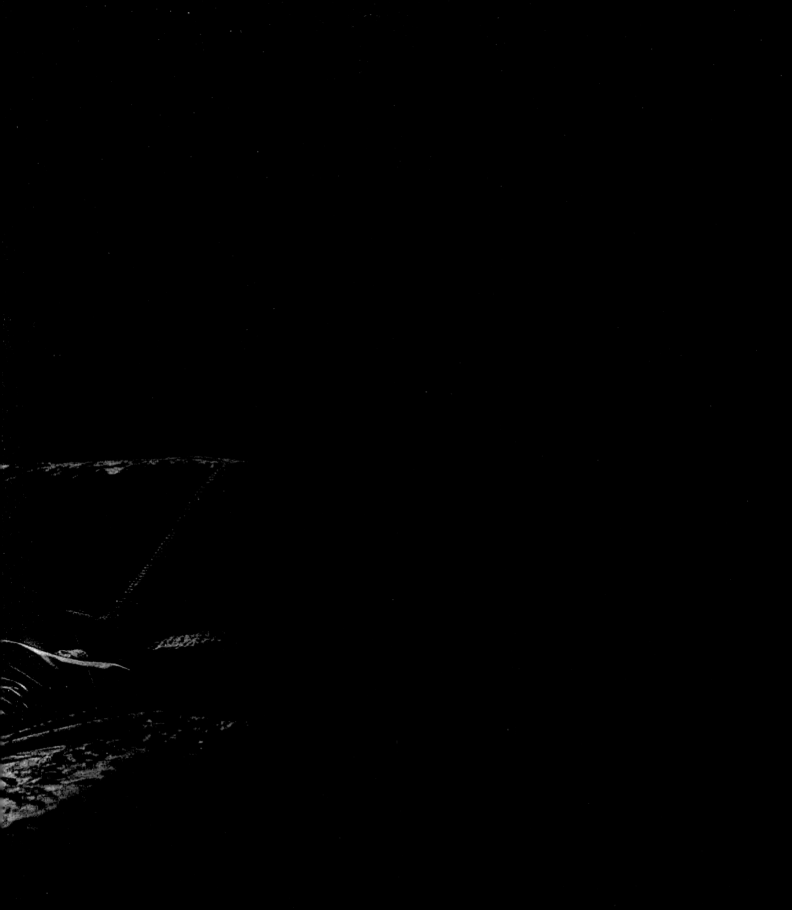

in her voice, perhaps they were listening for the wrong things. Many make the mistake of assuming passion can be conveyed only by singers with the lungpower to deliver a song at maximum volume – a notion promoted today by shows like *The X-Factor*, which pick winners based on how loudly they sing.

Madonna wasn't that sort of belter; thus, her lack of range would always be misconstrued by some as lack of feeling. But, even bearing that in mind, it's difficult to see how anyone could have listened to *Like a Prayer* and not thought it her most expressive performance yet. The vocals were considerably stronger and deeper than on the previous records, and there was no mistaking the depth of her feelings – her "conviction", if you will. She would never have the biggest bark, but when it came to singing a song meaningfully, her vocals on 'Like a Prayer' can't be faulted.

That said, *Trouser Press* did hit the nail on the head in its description of the Madonna/Prince duet, 'Love Song'. It was one of two tracks Prince played on – the other being 'Act of Contrition' – and the magazine wasn't wrong in complaining that it "never gets off the ground". Judging by its place in the track listing – third, straight after the powerhouse opening punch of 'Like a Prayer' and 'Express Yourself' – it was intended as a key number, but it was neither artist's finest moment. Prince is the dominant party during its near-five-minutes of lazy funk riffs and ambling grooves, and Madonna gamely adds funky ad libs and a few lines in French, but between the pair of them, they manage only to persuade the listener that two of the great icons of the day were a bit bored in the studio one afternoon. What could they have made of the song if they had really put their backs into it?

Six singles were taken from *Like a Prayer* (though one, 'Dear Jessie', was released only outside the US). As with singles from prior LPs, they came out one on top of another, with scarcely a gap between the moment one faded and the next began its chart climb. It says something about the quality of the music she was making, however, that even the final singles of the run ('Dear Jessie', 'Keep it Together') didn't feel (too much) like attempts to squeeze the last drops out of the LP. Moreover, the first two (the title track and 'Express Yourself') were as powerful as anything Madonna had ever released, and the

middle pair, 'Oh Father' and 'Cherish', were a high-quality ballad and dance number, respectively.

After the title song, the funk-infused 'Express Yourself' was the biggest hit, reaching Number 2 and becoming an instant anthem. Its empowerment theme, which rousingly counselled women not to compromise in love, was reinforced by a video based on Fritz Lang's *Metropolis*. This was a stunning piece of film, and so it should have been for the reputed $5 million cost: the heavily symbolic storyline featured Madonna playing a boss of enslaved young men and then becoming a slave herself, in a futuristic setting and saturated colours (she was the only character photographed in colour). *Billboard* magazine voted it Best Music Video of 1989, and it won three MTV Awards (for all its notoriety, the 'Like a Prayer' video received few MTV nominations and won just one, Viewers' Choice).

All six singles from the album sold well except 'Oh Father', which got no higher than Number 20 in the American chart. It was the first time since 'Holiday' that she'd missed the Top 10 (which wouldn't happen again until 1993, when 'Bad Girl', from *Erotica*, peaked at Number 36), but the relatively low placing could hardly have been unexpected. 'Oh Father' was the bleakest song she had ever released, a disquietingly personal analysis of her relationship with Tony Ciccone. At the same time, the lyric expressed her anger at his behaviour after her mother died – in the video, it's depicted as a father shouting at his small daughter and tearing off her necklace.

The tune was slow and sombre, and the video drenched in sadness. Filmed in black and white, it showed the moment of her mother's death and her father's displaced anguish. Many of the scenes took place in a cemetery, in falling snow, and even though it ended on a positive note, with father and daughter meeting at her mother's graveside, it proved too desolate for record buyers.

As 1989 ended, Madonna's place in popular culture was acknowledged with a slew of end-of-decade awards. She was named Artist of the Decade by MTV, *People* magazine cited her as one of the 20 Who Defined the Decade (it also found space for her in a list called 25 Most Intriguing

"It's a relic of a time when pop stars didn't hang on the approval of their publicists before talking." *Rich Juzwiak*

People in the World for 1989) and she was ranked as one of the Top 20 Pop Artists of the 80s by the *Los Angeles Times*. *Rolling Stone*'s readers, meanwhile, continued their anti-Madonna campaign by voting her Worst Female Singer, but that only reaffirmed her significance.

She saw out 1989 by rehearsing for a 57-date world tour, officially titled Blond Ambition World Tour, but generally remembered as The One With the Conical Bra. The garment – actually a boned pink-satin leotard with suspenders, designed by Jean-Paul Gaultier – became so identified with her that, as with the Boy Toy belt, a version is now available online, price £24. It seems to be a must for professional impersonators, too. (The photos of women wearing it prove how tricky it is to pull off an angular, confrontational costume with authority; Madonna is perhaps the only person who could inhabit the leotard with the necessary mix of hauteur and sass.)

Blond Ambition was a multi-purpose tour, promoting both *Like a Prayer* and the soundtrack album *I'm Breathless* (the music from her latest film, *Dick Tracy*, which came out in June 1990, halfway through the tour). It was also filmed for what would become the 1991 documentary *Madonna: Truth or Dare* (known outside America as *In Bed with Madonna*). *Truth or Dare* delivered on its title: it showed the unvarnished Madonna, insofar as any representation of her could be called "unvarnished". Director Alek Keshishian accompanied the tour around the world, and his backstage and hotel footage revealed some fascinatingly unguarded moments.

The film showed her having a spat with her *Dick Tracy* co-star (and then-boyfriend), Warren Beatty, over her constant need to be in the spotlight; in another scene, she met an old school friend and awkwardly refused to be her baby's godmother; elsewhere, chatting with close friend Sandra Bernhard about which celebrity she would most like to meet, she was self-absorbed as only enormously famous people can be. These glimpses didn't always flatter her, but they made compelling viewing. Looking back on it in 2012, Rich Juzwiak of *Gawker* encapsulated its appeal: "It's a relic of a time before media training, when pop stars didn't hang on the approval of their publicists before talking."

Truth or Dare's success – it took over $3 million in its first weekend on general release – bore out the maxim that there's no such thing as bad publicity (or, at least, bad onscreen portrayals). If anything, it was almost a companion piece to the *Like a Prayer* album – both showed the woman behind the fame, and in both cases she wasn't always easy to love.

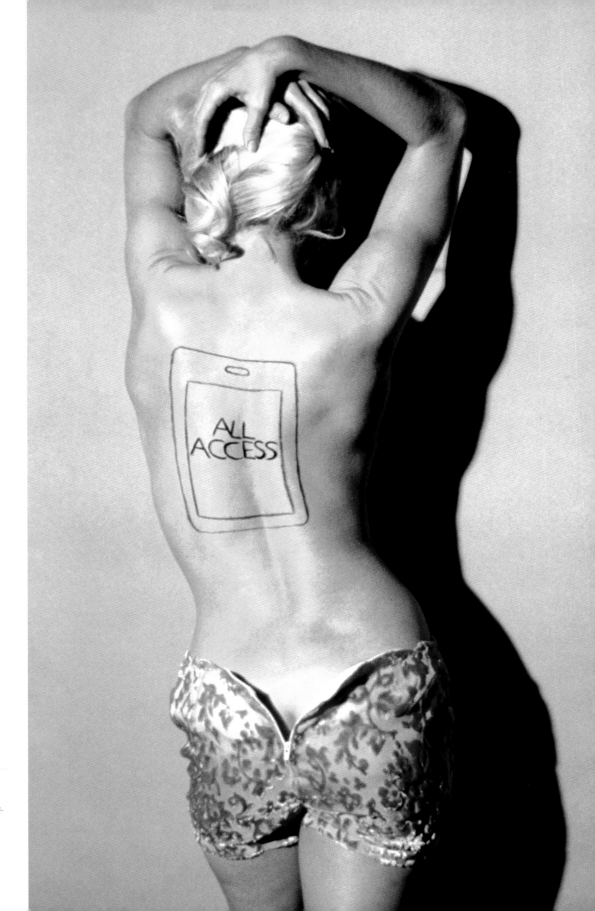

Left: Madonna at a tribute to Andrew Lloyd Webber in Los Angeles in 1991, five years before she starred in his *Evita*.

Right: A 1991 publicity still for *Truth or Dare*, which did indeed provide access to most areas of her life.

CHAPTER 6
EROTICA

The clue is in the title: Erotica *was Madonna's exploration of sex of all stripes, and used emphatic house and new jack swing grooves to propel her message along. Her candour, and Mistress Dita dominatrix persona, proved too much for some, as its mere 6 million sales proved.*

The release of *Erotica* and the book *Sex* marked the most controversial year of Madonna's career.

EROTICA

Her against the world: Introducing her alter ego Mistress Dita, Madonna releases Erotica *and* Sex, *the most controversial projects of her career. It's her gone-too-far moment, and the American public turns its back.*

It's impossible to discuss Madonna's fifth album without also considering *Sex*, the book she published on October 21, 1992, one day after the release of *Erotica*. Together, they launched the most divisive period of her career, and she paid for it with a marked dip in sales. Her 1993 film *Body of Evidence*, an erotic thriller in the style of *Basic Instinct*, could also be seen as part of this wave of carnally inspired projects. (It received scathing reviews and is little remembered today.)

Few would have predicted that *Erotica* would be her least successful album up to that point (relatively speaking: it still sold 6 million, but was a disappointment compared to *Like a Prayer*'s 15 million). As she began work on it, in June 1992, the portents actually pointed to her outdoing *Like a Prayer*. Her career was in excellent fettle: Blond Ambition had been voted 1990's top tour by *Rolling Stone*, and, also in 1990, she'd released two of her biggest singles – the non-album cuts 'Vogue' and 'Justify My Love'.

'Vogue' (from *I'm Breathless*, the soundtrack album inspired by the film *Dick Tracy*) was a particular triumph – selling six million, it put gay "ball" culture under the spotlight and is considered ground-breaking to this day. Meanwhile, 'Justify My Love' (released only on the 1990 greatest hits compilation *The Immaculate Collection*) sold a million in its own right. That was significant, because this whispery,

spoken-word number was an advance taste of the graphic ideas that would soon be heard throughout *Erotica*. If Americans would send an explicitly sexual track like 'Justify My Love' to the top of the chart, surely they would welcome an entire album of roughly the same sort of thing. And there would be a stylish book, *Sex*, to accompany it: on paper, this looked like the multi-media event of the year.

Working with photographer Steven Meisel – a close friend since his *Like a Virgin* sleeve photo rocketed her career into another league – Madonna began putting together *Sex* in January 1992. It was a high-end project, as reflected by the team she recruited, which included a former art director of Italian *Vogue*, the makeup artist Francois Nars and, to pose with her in the photos, a gaggle of models and socialites. Rapper Vanilla Ice, a sometime boyfriend, was there, too – for "kitsch value", as Madonna put it.

Shooting in Miami and Manhattan, the team developed an anything-goes policy that yielded pictures of lesbian encounters, bondage, S&M paraphernalia, knives and complete nudity. According to *Entertainment Weekly*'s Giselle Benatar, "A can-you-

Above Right: Arriving at the launch party for *Sex*. Industria Superstudio, New York, October 1992.

Below Right: The album was a manifesto whose basic principle was that everyone had the right to sexual expression.

"Madonna doesn't need to do it, but she wants to push buttons. So she does."

Francois Nars

"Madonna wanted Erotica to have a raw edge to it, as if it were recorded in an alley at 123rd Street in Harlem"

Shep Pettibone

top-this? dynamic developed between Madonna and her crew," leading to antics like the day a naked Madonna decided to do photos in the street outside her house, causing passing motorists to nearly pile into each other. On another day, she wore a body stocking to drive to a pizzeria, where she peeled it off in front of the customers. "Madonna doesn't need to do it, but she wants to push buttons. So she does," Francois Nars told Benatar.

Madonna also wrote text for the book, some of it in the guise of "Mistress Dita", a fantasy dominatrix inspired by the German actress Dita Parlo. Her prose style was not only fruity but rather breathless, and many critics would take issue with it: a fragrant description of Madonna's sexual awakening, aged 14, was judged "horrifyingly cutesy" by the *Independent*'s Zoe Heller.

Once the photo sessions were completed and the book was at the printer's – it was an expensive process, employing metal for the cover and a sealed outer envelope made of mylar – she turned her attention to *Erotica*, which was to be finished in time to be launched at the same time as *Sex*.

She started the sessions for *Erotica* in June as head of her own company. In March, she'd signed a deal with Time Warner to create the Maverick entertainment group, which gave her autonomy over her output. Part of Maverick's remit was to generate non-music projects, like *Sex*; because she was in effect working for herself, rather than Warner Bros, she was able to hone *Sex* to her exact specifications. (In the event, Maverick made its greatest profit through its record division: in 1995, it signed Alanis Morissette, who had been turned

Left: Enjoying the after-party for the premiere of *A League of Their Own*, 1992.

Right: Some publications censored this image of her modelling for Jean Paul Gaultier, 1992.

down by every other label, and built her into one of the decade's great confessional singer-songwriters.)

Madonna knew even before the *Erotica* sessions began what sound she wanted. She'd outgrown the sleekness of her Los Angeles collaborations with Pat Leonard and craved something grittier. Shep Pettibone, who specialized in dance remixes and had remixed several of her 80s singles, was chosen to produce most of the record (a few tracks were overseen by funk/soul producer Andre Betts). Pettibone's presence accounts for the LP's dramatically different, house-music leanings. "Madonna wanted *Erotica* to have a raw edge to it, as if it were recorded in an alley at 123rd Street in Harlem," the producer wrote in Madonna's fan-club magazine, *Icon*.

Its beats and arrangements made it her most club-friendly record since her debut. She had always been intuitive about when it was time to change, and here she grasped that the way to stay relevant was to incorporate the rave and house that was transforming young people's listening habits. At that moment, 1992, she was on the cusp between the 80s, when she'd rewritten the pop rulebook, and the mid-90s, when the little girls who'd grown up listening to her, like the Spice Girls, would storm the charts. This would be, she must have known, her high-water mark as a pop transgressor, so she made it count.

It wasn't Pettibone's stark, bass-heavy songs that got the public talking – though there was much praise for "the bottom-heavy boom

of contemporary dance music", as singled out by J.D. Considine in the *Baltimore Sun*. It was the subject matter: Madonna had never before written so openly about sex. These weren't the cute come-hither ditties of the early years or stirring do-it-yourself anthems like 'Express Yourself'; these were expressions of desire that left nothing to the imagination.

The sleeve and booklet, photographed by Meisel, showed her in a state of heavy-lidded ecstasy. The cover was an extreme close-up of her face – eyes closed, mouth open, clearly in transports of lust. Inside, things were even more explicit: in one shot she was wearing leather cuffs and holding a riding crop; another showed her bound and gagged; in a third, someone's toe was crammed into her mouth; and in a fourth she was biting a nipple ring attached to a partner who was out of shot (and undoubtedly wincing). Most striking, though, were the photos that just showed her face: she looked exhausted, jaded, her thirst utterly slaked.

The opening track, 'Erotica', had her back in character as Mistress Dita. Speaking most of the lyric – only the choruses were sung – Madonna addressed a sexual partner, telling him about the pain she would soon be inflicting. She outlined what was expected – she was the boss, and the lover would passively accept whatever she did. She was chilly, aloof:

Above and Right: At contrast with her *Erotica*/*Sex* book image, Madonna looking radiant on the beach, where her vintage clothes and pearls impart Monroe-ish glamour.

"I never show any unsafe sex, so I'm not promoting unsafe sex" Madonna

In one of the more charged exchanges of the interview, Blame earnestly asked whether it was right to release a video that "glamorized" sex but failed to include a safe-sex message. She patiently replied, "In the video I never show any unsafe sex, so I'm not promoting unsafe sex. If someone puts a harness on me and is riding me around like a farm animal, I don't consider that unsafe sex." And she was right – 'Erotica' may have promoted seediness and nudity but only the most determined moralist would claim it encouraged risky behaviour, Unless wearing a harness and being ridden by twelve stone of beefcake counts as dangerous.

Nonetheless, its overall atmosphere was dangerously dark. This was two decades before *Fifty Shades of Grey* made sadomasochism a water-cooler topic, and the riding crops and harnesses opened a window on behaviour that had rarely been covered in pop songs, and certainly never this openly. And the rest of the album was similarly inclined, focusing on sex in the most confrontational way. 'Where Life Begins', also intoned in a frigid, half-spoken style, invited listeners to consider what it would be like to perform oral sex on her, while 'Secret Garden' was a homage to, what else, a part of her own body.

Yet none of it sounded very sexy; she was too blank, too controlling. Even the album's conventional love songs – 'Rain', 'Waiting', 'Bye Bye Baby' – felt impersonal. 'Bye Bye Baby', in fact, mirrored the detachment of Debbie Harry at her Blondie peak. Its story of ditching some idiot after he failed to appreciate her for the thousandth time was delivered with the amused irony that was Harry's stock in trade. "Bye bye!" Madonna said brightly as the song ended, informing her Mr Wrong that she had bigger fish to fry.

The song in which she was most "there" was 'In This Life', a tribute to friends she had lost to AIDS. Her sincerity was unmistakeable, and the tune was raw with empathy. It was *Erotica*'s morning-after comedown, acknowledging that unbridled sexual freedom could exact an awful price.

When the album was released, critics didn't know what to make of it. You could almost see the giggling embarrassment as they tried to address the BDSM aspect, with numerous japes about "pain" and "kink". The most pungent summing-up came from *Stylus* magazine's Alfred Soto in 2006: "*Erotica* is Madonna's *120 Days of Sodom* as written by a woman with a bathetic Catholic streak."

it was easy to picture her sitting on a throne, incuriously eyeing some cowering supplicant. The Velvet Underground's 'Venus in Furs' had described this scenario from the male submissive's viewpoint; now here was the female dominant's response. Pettibone's minimal electronic beats (and a sample from Kool and The Gang's 'Jungle Boogie', of all things) added a sinister top layer to the swirling dark cloud.

And then there was the video. This was shown only three times on MTV, and then only after midnight, but it's surprising the channel risked it at all. The video was essentially a succession of images designed to shock (or make the viewer pull their chair closer to the TV). Madonna played a masked dominatrix who found herself surrounded by riding crops, tongues and bare bosoms – so much flesh, so little time to explore it all. In the European version, unreleased in America, it ended with a frontal shot of a naked Madonna standing in the street. And, in case it wasn't clear what this was about, the letters S E X flashed up.

The clip teetered between soft-core porn and art house fantasy. Too arty to be proper pornography – filmed in black-and-white, and everyone dazzlingly beautiful – it was also too X-rated to pass for family entertainment. In an interview with MTV's Steve Blame, Madonna mused that she'd released the album at "a very moralistic time" in America. Her hope was that the video might help to persuade the public to be tolerant of others' sexual preferences.

Left: After Blond Ambition Madonna said she would never tour again, but three years later she hit the road with the Girlie Show Tour.

Right: Madonna on stage at Wembley Stadium, London, where the 39-date Girlie Show spectacular kicked off.

It says something about the album's shock value that, even today, *Erotica* is seen as a paradigm of smuttiness. Reviewing a new Beyoncé album in January 2014, the *Daily Telegraph*'s Neil McCormick had to go all the way back to *Erotica* to find a comparison. "The bulk of the album is X-rated stuff, perhaps the rudest mainstream pop album since Madonna's *Erotica*." Back in 1992, would Madonna have thought it was all worthwhile if she had known that her work would be remembered simply as "rude mainstream pop"?

The question many critics asked, in one form or another, was: how much further could she go without losing fans? They soon got their answer.

The day after *Erotica* came out, *Sex* hit the bookshops. Each spiral-bound book came with a comic and a CD, the whole thing encased in silver mylar packaging modelled on – what else? – condom wrappers. A single run of one million copies had been printed, with no more to follow; despite some shops restricting sales to over-18s and a hefty price tag – $49.99 in the US; £30 in the UK – the entire run quickly sold out. Judging by the number of pristine copies available on eBay, some bought the book purely as an investment. One such, on offer for $495.00, is accompanied by a blurb that declares, "It is numbered and STILL SEALED in Bag. The Condition is FLAWLESS! It looks like it was just released."

Nearly $500 may seem a swingeing sum, flawless or not, but, as the seller says, "After 20 years it is STILL the #1 Most Collectible Book of All Time." That's not an exaggeration. The site BookFinder. com lists it as the most searched for out-of-print book in the USA – despite one seller warning that the mylar envelope disintegrates once opened. It wouldn't be surprising if even the disintegration had been part of the plan; every facet of *Sex* had been calibrated to be a talking point.

"Madonna is both the medium and the message. We know it's gonna be controversial and it's gonna sell books," Nanscy Neiman of Warner's publishing division told Michael Gross in an interview in *New York* magazine just before publication. The whole project was taken so seriously that when Gross asked, possibly facetiously, whether *Sex* would have an effect on the upcoming US presidential election, Neiman's eyes apparently "lit up". Maybe *Sex* did wield some subliminal power; Bill Clinton ended up in the White House two weeks later, ending 12 years of Republican rule.

So *Sex* was an unqualified commercial success. Critically, it was a different story. Reviewers piled in to slate it. Criticism was divided into two schools of thought: the smut school, so to speak, condemned it as pornography; the rest were simply disappointed that the photos were so unsexy.

Some critics contended that, despite all the build-up, *Sex* wasn't very Sex-y. It was a sentiment repeated in John Leland's *Newsweek* review, which found the book "cold and uninviting, pushing you away rather than drawing you in". Even a cover story in *Vanity Fair* called it "perhaps the dirtiest coffee-table book ever published" (which was, to be fair, more a description than a judgment).

Madonna and her team were prepared for all this. "There's a lot to hate in that book," her publicist Liz Rosenberg admitted to journalist Maureen Orth in the same *Vanity Fair* piece, while Madonna said matter-of-factly, "I don't have the same hang-ups that other people do, and that's the point I'm trying to make with this book."

And she made it – vociferously and once and for all. It would be interesting to know what response she'd expected. Her business was pushing society's buttons, but was she really surprised that the

> # *"If someone puts a harness on me and is riding me around like a farm animal, I don't consider that unsafe sex."*
>
> *Madonna*

feedback was so negative? And, for some, it wasn't even the nudity and nipple rings but her righteous tone – here she was, publishing an entire book to tell people how to be sexually free.

The consensus was that Madonna had gone too far; the warm spirituality of *Like a Prayer* had been superseded by something that was cold and hard to embrace. The warmer Madonna wouldn't return until *Ray of Light* in 1998; for now, she had committed herself to a course as an extreme provocateur, pushing fringe sex as just another lifestyle choice. (Many reviewers also worried about what her young fan base would think of all the "sexual hoo-ha"; years later, several writers would reminisce about having read the book when they were 13 or 14 – and admit that they found it thoroughly confusing.)

The negativity had its effect. Though the book sold out, the publicity overshadowed the *Erotica* album, keeping it from properly taking off. It was hardly a flop, reaching Number 2 and eventually selling six million copies worldwide, but by her standards, this was disappointing. Nor did its singles gain traction, except on the club chart. In the mainstream US Top 100, only the title track and 'Deeper and Deeper' reached the Top 10 – and those two songs are the only ones generally remembered today.

A backlash developed, the Vatican banning her from entering its precincts, and Lebanon and China banning the album. Previously, controversy had been one of her main drivers of sales; now it was having

the opposite effect. And when the film *Body of Evidence* came out, in January 1993, critics were spurred to greater heights of negativity.

She played an art dealer accused of murdering her wealthy older lover, and Willem Dafoe played her lawyer. The focus of the story was a sadomasochistic relationship between the pair – she tied him up, poured hot wax all over his body and engaged in other activities that would have been familiar to anyone who owned a copy of *Sex*. Coming on the heels of *Sex* and *Erotica*, the film convinced some reviewers that she was now mainly about pornography – anticipating this, producer Dino de Laurentiis was said to have asked her to delay the release of *Sex* so it wouldn't be seen as "the *Sex* movie".

Most of the criticism, though, was simply directed at what the *Chicago Tribune*'s Gene Siskel called a "stupid and empty" story. "More silly than erotic" was *Variety*'s opinion, while others noted that casting Madonna alongside heavyweight actors such as Dafoe and Joe Mantegna "revealed [her] inability to project any depth or sense of real emotion", as Chris Hicks of the *Deseret News* put it.

The role "won" her another Razzie for Worst Actress; undaunted, she began shooting a new movie, *Dangerous Game*, just a month after

---

Left: Performing 'Like a Virgin' as an homage to Marlene Dietrich, complete with German accent.

Above: A peepshow-type display outside a Manhattan bookshop in the run-up to the publication of *Sex*, October 1992.

Body of Evidence appeared. This would actually earn her some of her most positive reviews; playing an actress who drives a director to commit suicide, her effort was lauded by the showbiz bible *Variety* as one of her best showings yet. The film was, however, a box-office flop. In a 2002 interview with Scott Tobias of AVClub.com, its director, Abel Ferrara speculated that, good reviews or no, Madonna wasn't confident enough in front of the camera. "[And] if you don't have confidence, the camera sees that and comes barrelling through."

To promote *Erotica*, Madonna set out in September 1993, on her fourth tour, The Girlie Show. It was the usual continent-roving spectacular, with, aptly, a "sex circus" theme – a cross between a burlesque show, a cabaret and a gig, with the sort of set pieces that were unique to Madonna gigs. The opening number featured a topless dancer (later, during 'Fever', Madonna herself partially stripped); 'Like a Virgin' was a camp 1930s spoof, with the singer dressed in top hat and tails and singing in a German accent; during 'The Beast Within' there was a homoerotic "fight" between the male dancers; 'Bye Bye Baby' included faux-lesbian dominatrix action with a female dancer.

Just the average Madonna gig, then: titillation mixed with old-fashioned entertainment. The production values, naturally, were very high; some of the sets, designed by her brother Christopher, evoked classic MGM musicals, while others recreated the glittering heyday of Studio 54. Obviously, there were a few stop-press incidents: the Tel Aviv gig, her first ever in Israel, was the subject of protests by Orthodox Jews; and at the show in Puerto Rico, she antagonized the country's government by sliding the national flag between her legs. The Puerto Rican House of Representatives passed a motion censuring her, and Florida-based Puerto Ricans gathered outside her house in Miami and destroyed CDs – though she wasn't there to witness it, as she was playing in Rio De Janeiro that day.

The 39 dates, which wound up just before Christmas with five nights at the 42,000-capacity Tokyo Dome, would be her last until 2001. The tour wasn't an unqualified success; critic Jon Pareles likened it to a variety show, musing that it would have worked equally well in Las Vegas. A fittingly ambivalent conclusion to the most controversial year of Madonna's career.

CHAPTER 7
BEDTIME STORIES

After the rawness of Erotica, Bedtime Stories offered a more sensual take on sex. Deep bass grooves (and some of the biggest producers in R&B) enticed fans back to the fold.

Madonna's soft *Bedtime Stories* look was a deliberate contrast to *Erotica's* Mistress Dita persona.

BEDTIME STORIES

Bedtime Stories' *quiet-storm R&B enables Madonna to repair her reputation after the public condemnation of* Erotica. *But David Letterman picks a fight, and she rises to the occasion.*

"Making this album was a true test of my sanity and stability," Madonna wrote in the credits section of *Bedtime Stories*. If that sounds dramatic, read the lyrics to the 11 songs on her sixth album. Riven with heartache and disquiet, they add up to the most troubled album she's ever made. The titles reflect her state of mind: 'Survival', 'Sanctuary', 'Love Tried to Welcome Me' ("tried" rather than "did"). There was little happiness, almost no optimism. But here's the perverse thing: sonically, this was one of her prettiest and most emollient albums.

It was as if Madonna had decided that such bruised lyrics would be best offset by a soft, cushiony setting – the diametric opposite of *Erotica*'s chromium chill. To achieve it she assembled a new team of producers – but, rather than hiring the usual bubbling-under hipster, she called on the established talents of Dallas Austin, Dave "Jam" Hall and Babyface. All at the top of their game, they had more or less invented the lustrous R&B/new jack swing sound then dominating the airwaves. She also recruited British hotshot Nellee Hooper, one of the architects of trip hop, and then in great demand because of his work on Bjork's 1993 album, *Debut*. Producing a few tracks apiece, they created a creamy R&B sound that was as silky as *Erotica*'s electronic pulse had been hard.

There was a solid commercial reason for adopting R&B: it was the sound of the 90s, making stars of artists like Mary J Blige, Toni Braxton and TLC. But, in the main, it was an effort to draw a line under the *Erotica/Sex* period, the fallout from which was still affecting her. In an interview with *Spin*'s Bob Guccione Jr in late 1995, she would say: "I divide my career from before and after the *Sex* book. Very few people came to my rescue. It was an incredibly eye-opening experience."

She addressed the experience on *Bedtime Stories* with a song called 'Human Nature'. It hit her detractors head-on, angrily defending her right to freedom of speech. It was one of the record's most powerful tracks, its message delivered in a flatly accusatory style; essentially, she refused to apologize or be shamed for having talked about sex. If people didn't like it, she not only didn't care, she took pleasure in watching them squirm. The venom in her voice as she half-sang, half-whispered would have felled the most sanctimonious censor.

That the album was called *Bedtime Stories* – alluding again to physical appetites – must have inflamed her enemies' sensibilities still further. This time, though, her idea of bedtime was a more sensual, subtle affair. The sleeve photo (taken by Patrick Demarchelier, the latest in a long line of fashion photographers to shoot her covers) set a scene that was very different from *Erotica*'s black-PVC nightscape. The cover was

Right: With nightclub owner Ingrid Casares (centre) at actor Wesley Snipes's birthday party in 1994.

Right: Looking suitably glamorous, Madonna posing with friend at a Jean Paul Gaultier fashion show in 1994.

"I divide my career from before and after the Sex book. Very few people came to my rescue. It was an incredibly eye-opening experience."

Madonna

"You can't get through a show without talking about me."

Madonna, to David Letterman

all tumbled blond curls, frothy white lace and winsome smiles, while the inside pictures had her tumbling around in a white negligée in a jade-green hotel room. The effect was innocently seductive, far more Marilyn Monroe than Mistress Dita. If there was a subtext, it was: kinkiness is all very well, but sometimes vanilla is more fun.

When she started composing the album, early in 1994, her intention had been to reprise *Erotica*'s bass-heavy clubbiness. Shep Pettibone had again been her choice of producer, but, at some point early in the project, she decided to soften her approach. Pettibone was no longer involved – "Thanx to Shep Pettibone for being understanding," she wrote in the credits – and the R&B-oriented quartet of Babyface, Austin, Hall and Hooper were in.

'Human Nature', co-produced by Hall, was one of just two tracks that alluded to the messiness surrounding *Sex* and *Erotica*. The other was 'Survival', which was about exactly that – being stoic in the face of condemnation, in the knowledge that right is on your side. Most of the other songs were pensive meditations on love, steeped in an unfamiliar uncertainty and yearning – and then there was the singular track called 'Bedtime Story'. Written by rising Icelandic star Bjork, it was a hypnotic abstraction of a tune with a slow-pulsing trip-hop beat. In typical Bjorkean fashion, the lyric wandered into hazy, psychedelic realms, toying with the idea that spoken language was redundant and should be replaced by "unconsciousness". According to Bjork, Madonna actually got the words slightly wrong: "She did her own version and wrote the lyrics wrong. I can't remember right now, but it was a really interesting mistake," she told *Attitude* magazine.

Madonna's drowsy sighs and purrs brought the song vividly to life: who indeed needed language when unconsciousness was so seductive? The song would prove too odd for most tastes, though, and only the support of her hardore fans got it into the American chart, where it peaked at Number 42 – the first time she had missed the US Top 40 since 'Burning Up' in 1983. In the UK, which had always been supportive, it reached Number 4. (Over the next few years, Britain would emerge as her most reliable market; even singles that were unsuccessful elsewhere sailed into the UK Top 20, indicating an intriguing difference in national musical tastes.)

She cut a prickly, troubled figure during this period. That much was obvious from an appearance on David Letterman's chat show in March 1994, an experience that was memorable for both herself and Letterman. In her defence, it must be said that Letterman was the instigator of the antagonistic exchange that followed. He went beyond the bounds of accepted "edginess" from the start by introducing her as a woman who had "slept with some of the biggest names in the entertainment industry". From that moment, the interview went irretrievably off track.

This was Letterman's way of needling a cultural monolith whose career seemed to be on the slide, and she responded in the way she knew would irk him most – by peppering the conversation with so much swearing that viewers would complain in their droves. Within two minutes, she dropped the first F-word – "You know, you are a sick fuck," she told him, smiling as he winced – and it went on from there.

She handed him a pair of knickers – not the ones she was wearing – and invited him to smell them. She swore a bit more; she made a smutty joke about the overhead microphone. "This is American television," Letterman protested. "You can't be coming on here and talking about that." The rest of their 20 minutes together was a grudge match of puerile barbs. He referred suggestively to her (platonic) relationship with basketball player Charles Barkley (she was actually dating another NBA star, Dennis Rodman); she showed what she thought of that by swearing lustily. She asked if he was wearing a toupée; referring to her tightly pulled-back hair, he shot back, "Are you wearing a swim cap?" Throughout, she fidgeted and giggled, warning several times, "Don't fuck with me".

It was a textbook example of a TV host losing control of his interview, and it can't be said that he didn't deserve it. If anything, this was his comeuppance for having made endless jokes about her over the years. That was what riled her most: "All you do is talk about my sex life on your show," she said. "You can't get through a show without talking about me."

Afterward? When the programme was shown, its viewing figures were among the highest in its history. Madonna, meanwhile, was

rewarded with what she called "the entire nation beating up on [me]". The response, reflected in complaints to the Federal Communications Commission, was the clearest sign yet that (some of) the American public had had enough. The public condemnation "intimidated" her, she told *Spin*'s Guccione nearly two years later. She'd admitted she regretted doing the Letterman show; the public response had taken her by surprise. Nonetheless, she maintained that Letterman had been rude to her, so her behaviour had been justified. Anyway, why was it acceptable to show violence on TV, but ostracize her for swearing?

The *Spin* interview is an interesting snapshot of her life in late 1995, 13 years into her recording career. It took place in London, where she was recording the soundtrack to *Evita*, the film that would finally force critics to take her seriously as an actress. Talking to Guccione, she wore a yoke of persecution, at one point even likening herself to oppressed social groups. Everyone was afraid of strong women like her, she claimed, which made her "identify" with other minorities. She even wondered, in all earnestness, why "the black community" wasn't as supportive as she had expected.

As silly as that sounds, it's hard not to sympathize with her, given the lack of respect she often encountered. Later in the interview, for instance, she was asked how she felt about a recent story in *Buzz* magazine that described sleeping with her as the "uncoolest" experience anyone could have. It was an unpleasant, judgmental question – how would anyone feel about it? – but her graceful response was that there was nothing she could do to change some people's thoughts.

Everything that was going on in early 1994, then, informed her approach to *Bedtime Stories*. Despite the expletives displayed to Letterman, she was set on repairing her image. Thus, her original plan to make another record in the aloof electronic mode of *Erotica* went by the wayside, and in came Austin, Babyface, Hooper and Hall with their warm, organic styles. But even before the album sessions started, she'd released the first salvo of her reinvention campaign.

'I'll Remember' (full title 'I'll Remember: Theme from the Motion Picture *With Honors*') was her first single of 1994, and doesn't appear on any of her albums, other than a 1995 collection of ballads, *Something to Remember*. Musically a throwback to her early days, it was a straightforwardly romantic synth-pop ditty. Her film songs had

"If I used your fingers... it's sexual abuse."

Madonna

always been strong sellers – 'Crazy for You' from *Vision Quest*, 'Who's That Girl' from the film of that name and 'Vogue' from *Dick Tracy* had all reached Number 1 – and her label decided that the best way to test the water was by putting out another.

To create the song, she reunited with Pat Leonard, producer of *True Blue* and *Like a Prayer*. The result was sweet and uncomplicated: singing at the lower end of her register, as she typically did on ballads, she mourned the end of a love affair to a low-key synth arrangement. It was emotional but not overwrought, and the melody pretty but not sugary. (A noteworthy bit of miscellany is that the American maxi-single version contains a remix by William Orbit, who would produce her career-transforming 1998 album, *Ray of Light*. He used a light touch on 'I'll Remember', adding a sparkling ambient atmosphere that in retrospect was the obvious precursor to *Ray of Light*.)

Its video was more ambiguous: decked out like a 30s film star, with a glossy black bob and pencil-thin eyebrows, she was pictured in a recording studio, being directed by a shadowy figure behind a mixing desk. Scenes from *With Honors* played on a screen behind her. As the video ended, the figure was revealed as Madonna herself, wearing a man's coat – the kind of role-reversal playfulness she just couldn't resist.

With Honors – in which she didn't appear – was a flop; the single, by contrast, returned her to the chart in great style. It rose to Number 2 in

the US and stayed there for four weeks, kept off the top spot only by the R&B quartet All-4-One, whose single 'I Swear' was halfway through an 11-week run at Number 1. It was further validated by a Number 1 placing in the US Adult Contemporary chart, as well as Golden Globes and Grammy nominations.

This laid the groundwork for the release of *Bedtime Stories* in October. In the interim, she made up with Letterman. The two appeared at the MTV Awards (presenting the Video of the Year statuette to Aerosmith), all rancour conspicuously absent. They arrived onstage arm-in-arm to a standing ovation, and as they reached the podium, she joked, "And you thought we wouldn't last!"

And then Aerosmith clambered onstage to collect their award and did their best to humiliate her. "Madonna, baby!" exclaimed singer Steve Tyler, the very picture of dudely machismo. "Why do you use these two fingers [flexing his own fingers] to masturbate with?" Nonplussed, she simply stared at him. "Because they're mine!" he crowed.

She pushed her way back to the microphone and snapped, "If I used your fingers, then it's not masturbation" – pause – "it's sexual abuse." It was a repellent scene: Tyler and his band mates milling around,

Left: Madonna takes centre stage the Gaultier show. *Bedtime Stories* was about to come out, so what better way of publicizing it?

Above: Embracing Jean Paul Gaultier in New York at the launch of one of his perfumes, September 1994.

123

trying to shame her because – it was obvious from Tyler's expression – she deserved it. Madonna's answering quip was snappy enough, and she was generally seen as having got the better of him, but it was a depressing encounter nonetheless.

A few days later, *Bedtime Stories'* lead single, 'Secret', came out. It was the first of her singles to be available as a download as well as on the usual formats. Clunky mid-90s technology made it difficult to access online, but those who persevered were able to download not just the single but a message from Madonna, which began, "Hello, all you cyberheads!" The rest of her message suggested that she had grasped the possibilities of the internet as a promotional tool. "Welcome to the 90s version of intimacy," she went on. "You can hear me, you can see me, but you can't touch me." After plugging *Bedtime Stories*, which was due a month later, she announced that the 'Secret' video, which she'd just filmed, would also be available to watch online.

She was one of the first artists to use the internet this way. At 36, she was of the pre-internet generation but smoothly incorporated the digital world into her promotional armoury, realizing it was the best way to reach younger fans, who were starting to congregate online in large numbers.

The download release didn't count toward chart sales, but the physical version sold enough to reach Number 3. The understated feel of the track was complemented by the video, a black-and-white clip filmed in Harlem. She played a singer in an African-American nightclub, dreamily drifting through the streets, past shoppers, street-kids and cross-dressers putting on their wigs. Eventually – the only white person in the video – she arrived home to her black husband and baby, turning to smile at the camera as the clip faded. It was soft and sensuous, but also guaranteed to raise eyebrows: again portraying herself as a "minority" and aligning herself with a similarly "oppressed" group, she was daring the American mainstream to take offence.

Few did. The tune was beguiling enough in its own right to be appreciated purely on its musical merits. (*Slant* magazine would declare it one of the 100 best singles of the 90s.) When *Bedtime Stories* followed, on October 25, she had amassed enough good will to receive generally positive reviews.

Teaming up with Austin, Babyface and the rest had worked the magic she needed. Here was a record filled with quiet-storm ballads and slow jams, and even if these didn't push the sonic envelope as *Erotica* had, they were very much in keeping with what young Americans were listening to. That was important; she wasn't an "albums artist", who could plough her own musical furrow without worrying about selling singles. For her, singles were key, and they had to be hits; without them, the LPs wouldn't take off. So it was vital that *Bedtime Stories* produced radio-friendly tracks, and in late 1994, the best way to ensure that was to go the R&B/new-jack route.

Consider the American charts in the week *Bedtime Stories* came out. Among the Top 10 singles were Boyz II Men's smoochy smash hit 'I'll Make Love to You' (produced, coincidentally, by Babyface); Aaliyah's seductive 'At Your Best'; the R&B trio Immature's 'Never Lie'; and Babyface himself with the acoustic-soul ballad 'When Can I See You'. Thus, with *Bedtime Stories*, Madonna was in the right place at the right time.

This isn't to imply that her adoption of new-jack/jill swing was entirely calculated. A case could even be made for the notion that her very first album was a forerunner of the genre: its aesthetic was the same, with dance beats underpinning lyrics that saw both romance and the steamiest sex as themes that could be addressed in the same song.

"Welcome to the 90s version of intimacy,"

Madonna

Bedtime Stories featured fewer melodies than before, and more of an emphasis on grooves, with head-spinning basslines at the forefront. *Erotica* had also focused on the groove at the expense of melody; she was brave in moving yet further away from her catchy pop foundations. The reason Madonna had sold all those records in the 80s was that they were fiendishly infectious – her run of singles from 1983 to 1989 was pretty well second to none in terms of pure infectious pop brilliance. And now she was yanking the rug out from under her original fans' feet, cutting out the anthemic choruses and telling them to get into the groove instead.

That said, those 1984 Wannabes – the teenagers who had risked their parents' wrath by wearing fishnet tops and transparent bras – were adults now, and, traditionally, adults didn't buy singles. The fan base needed new seedlings, who had to be young enough to go to the record shop and hand over $2 for the song they'd just heard on the radio, rather than wait around for the album. Luckily, enough of them did that with 'Secret' to send it into the Top 5, and *Bedtime Stories* benefited, making its chart debut in early November at Number 3.

Reviews were almost uniformly warm, though a few complained about what they perceived as self-absorption. But most critics, thoughtfully contrasting the arrangements' lushness with the

forlornness of the lyrics, found much to praise. Although *Rolling Stone*'s Barbara O'Dair was disappointed that Madonna hadn't written a collection of feminist anthems in response to the slating she'd got for *Erotica*/*Sex* (only 'Human Nature' really came close, and that was a personal, not political, response), she conceded that the record was striking: it was, she said, an assertion that Madonna wasn't by any means finished with her work.

Entertainment Weekly was taken by the lyrics, noting that her writing style had changed from impersonal characterisations to something much more personal. The *Los Angeles Times*' Chris Willman agreed: "Here she returns to tender expressions of love and loneliness; yeah, the soft Madonna is back."

Despite the approval, *Bedtime Stories* didn't make a great commercial splash. It sold a global total of seven million copies, fewer than any of her albums except *Erotica*, *American Life*, *Hard Candy* and *MDNA*. But if it wasn't a blockbuster, it did produce one blockbuster song.

'Take a Bow', released as the second single in December, 1994, did what perhaps seemed impossible at that point: it became one of the biggest tracks of her career. It spent seven weeks at the top of the American chart – longer than any of her other singles ('Like a Virgin', at six weeks, is in second place) – and, for the first time in years, made her music a talking point for actual musical reasons.

In the UK, it reached only Number 16; as mentioned before, British record buyers had distinctly different preferences when it came to Madonna songs. Thus, they failed to be swept away by 'Take a Bow' but loved the next two singles, 'Bedtime Story' and 'Human Nature', propelling them into the Top 5, while in America these stalled outside the Top 40.

Madonna had always been a persuasive balladeer, and for Americans 'Take a Bow' – a Babyface co-write – pushed all the right buttons: it was tender and deeply melodic; a ready-made "our song" for couples. It took the Best Female Video trophy at the 1995 MTV Awards and was used in the first series of *Friends* – what greater sign that she had been accepted back into the fold? As ever, though, she was there on her own terms.

Above Left: Madonna relaxing at the Soul Train Awards with actress/dancer Rosie Perez, March 1994.

Above: Madonna at the MTV Awards, September 1994, where she presented the Best Video trophy to Aerosmith.

CHAPTER 8
RAY OF LIGHT

Madonna's major artistic statement: the 20 million-selling Ray of Light *took electronic music into the mainstream, while revealing a depth and spirituality generated by the birth of her first baby.*

The *Ray of Light* era, when Madonna reinvented herself as a honey-blonde, soft-featured earth mother.

RAY OF LIGHT

Motherhood and Kabbalah lead to a spiritual awakening
– and Ray of Light, *a career-changing artistic statement.*

By the time *Ray of Light* emerged in February 1998, her life had changed beyond measure. In October 1996, she had given birth to Lourdes Maria Ciccone Leon, her longed-for first child. "This is the greatest miracle of my life," she told *People* magazine's Todd Gold a few days afterward – and, as someone whose career had been touched by a number of miracles along the way, she was qualified to know.

Lourdes's father was Carlos Leon, a trainer she'd met in 1994, while jogging in Central Park; they separated in 1997 – "We're better off as best friends," she said – but remain close to this day. He and Lourdes (the name chosen to honour Madonna's mother, who had always wanted to visit the French shrine) have an equally strong relationship that has apparently been tested by his strictness as she's grown up. Madonna, the tabloids assure us, is the good cop, insofar as exercising leniency, while bad cop Leon lays down the law. His watchful approach has led to a spate of rather wonderful "Papa, don't preach" headlines.

Madonna had approached pregnancy with her usual rigorous discipline; until her eighth month, according to her personal trainer, Ray Kybartas, she'd worked out six times a week (just before giving birth, she was still managing three sessions per week).

Lourdes's birth had been preceded by an intensely busy nine months. Between February and May 1996, Madonna had filmed *Evita*, the role she'd wanted so badly that she'd written to director Alan Parker,

explaining why she would be perfect as Eva Duarte, wife of Argentine president Juan Peron. Parker recalled that "…she said that she would sing, dance and act her heart out, and put everything else on hold to devote all her time to it." Which she did, throwing herself into it so wholeheartedly that she was often sick.

Halfway through filming she'd learned she was pregnant. She found it both terrifying and euphoric; it was a pivotal moment for her life and her career. It was then, at a dinner party during her pregnancy, that she had her second profound awakening. She was introduced to Kabbalah, a new-age interpretation of Judaism, by Sandra Bernhard – and at that point, as she wrote in an article for the Israeli newspaper *Yediot Ahronot*, "all the puzzle pieces started falling into place". After attending her first class, she realized that "my life would never be the same".

Money and fame had brought little fulfilment, she said; life seemed like "a series of random events", and years of trying to centre herself by reading about Taoism, early Christianity and Buddhism had failed. Kabbalah was a kind of rebirth, and felt especially significant to her as the mother of a daughter. She felt the need to teach Lourdes a belief

Above Right: On the set of the 'Ray of Light' video, which won five MTV Awards in 1998.

Right: *Ray of Light* was partly inspired by the transformative effects of yoga and Kabbalah.

"All the puzzle pieces started falling into place".

Madonna

system, as her own mother had passed on her ardent Catholicism, and Kabbalah was the first faith she'd found that provided what she saw as the answers. Nearly 20 years later, her belief is still strong – she and her four children attend the Kabbalah Center in Manhattan, and boyfriends often accompany her as well.

Motherhood, *Evita*, Kabbalah – all informed her state of mind as she made *Ray of Light*. It was dramatically different, musically and thematically, from her other 90s albums (and from those that followed in the 2000s) – this was some of the most adventurous music she'd ever made. Plaudit was heaped on plaudit; her singing (much strengthened thanks to vocal training during *Evita*) and William Orbit's ambient/trip-hop/trance production were almost universally praised.

It won four Grammys, sold 20 million copies and topped the charts in a dozen countries (though not in America – there it debuted at Number 2, selling 370,000 copies in its first week, but was deprived of the top spot by the *Titanic* soundtrack). Crucially, too, it offered an elegant solution to the problem of how to compete with the much younger artists who were now dominating the charts (and who had grown up listening to her – without her, there would have been no Spice Girls). The answer, it seemed, had been staring her in the face: just act her age.

Ray of Light orchestrated her ultimate reinvention. Now there was no need to match starlets like Britney Spears on a "sexiness" level, because

her newfound spirituality gave her a gravitas that spoke directly to adult audiences. Now she was a seasoned performer, creating pop with depth. And she could use her experience to dispense big-sisterly wisdom to the likes of the Spice Girls, then the biggest female band in the world. "I like the Spice Girls," she told *Spin*'s Barry Walters. "Every time someone says something bad about them, I say, 'Hey, wait a minute, I was a Spice Girl once'." Indeed, she went to see them at Madison Square Garden in mid-1998, with 19-month-old Lourdes in tow (there's no record of Lourdes's reaction).

Ray of Light also introduced ambient music to the mainstream; Orbit's chilled, down tempo arrangements would be much emulated. For his part, he's always maintained that their collaboration was the turning point of his career – that she'd seen something in him that nobody else had and had given him the break he needed. Madonna's sleeve notes contain an affectionate tribute to him. Addressing him as Billy Bubbles, Madonna thanked him "for sharing my vision and daring to dream." She added, "Awright, geez, sorted, init", proving that even the most famous American woman in the word was girlishly susceptible to British men and their slang.

She began writing songs for *Ray of Light* in the spring of 1997, at first collaborating with Babyface. Teaming up with a former producer, then deciding to go a different way, was a Madonna hallmark; in this case, she decided the songs she was writing with Babyface had a 'Take a Bow' feeling that no longer felt right. Then there was a brief partnership with songwriter Rick Nowels, yielding several tracks that made it onto the album, including the future single 'The Power of Goodbye'. She also reunited with *True Blue/Like a Prayer* producer Pat Leonard, and got four songs from their sessions, among them 'Frozen', which would be the album's highest-charting single. Orbit was finally brought in at the suggestion of Guy Oseary, Maverick's chairman (and her future manager).

Orbit had remixed the 1994 single 'I'll Remember', and, conveniently, Madonna was a fan of his electronica/house fusion albums, *Strange Cargo* and *Strange Cargo II*; thus, they quickly gelled. The tracks she'd done with Nowels and Leonard were "slick", Orbit decided; his own approach was synth- and sample-led, with few live musicians involved. He worked with slivers of sounds – getting a live drummer into the studio, say, then chopping the sounds into bits to construct the tracks.

Madonna, meanwhile, wrote lyrics and melodies, and her ethereal compositions cleaved to Orbit's hypnotic soundscapes. "She's quite a vibe merchant – a real viber in the studio," Orbit said to *Keyboard* magazine a few months after the album's release. "Just letting things happen and keeping the vibe going." They were manifestly on the same wavelength; in their four months at Larrabee Studios North in Hollywood, they consistently "vibed" off each other, creating eight-minute trance tracks that they refined into three-minute pop songs. Like many of her past producers, he'd been impressed by how quickly she got things done in the vocal booth – once she'd written a lyric, she memorized it more or less on the spot, and when she started recording rarely needed more than a couple of takes.

Her lyrics reflected the transformation she had undergone. Many of *Ray of Light*'s songs are about her quest for enlightenment, right from the opening number, 'Drowned World/Substitute for Love'. It's one of the most public recantations of fame ever put to music. It starts as a delicate lullaby and expands into eerie trip-hop, speckled with jolts of drum & bass. Over this woozy backing, Madonna ruminates about celebrity – her "substitute for love". It's striking because it's so openly confessional: she sings about her craving for fame, and finding that all it brought was material things and boyfriends who had been there only for the reflected glory. Travelling around the world was an empty experience to her, and being the centre of attention was the worst kind of loneliness.

So it was depressing at the top – even for Madonna, the woman who had wanted to be there so desperately that she'd sacrificed love. It was the kind of midlife crisis only the super-famous could empathize with, and not everyone was kind; some critics decided she was simply showing off. Nonetheless, it was quite an admission, coming from someone who, in 1991, had told Martha Sherrill of the *Washington Post* that life was peachy, because she had "tons of money and tons of friends. What else do you need in life?" Just a year before that, she'd said more or less the same thing in a *Vanity Fair* interview with Kevin Sessums: "It's a great feeling to be powerful. I've been striving for it all my life."

Eight years later, motherhood was exerting a far greater influence: 'Drowned World' was also a paean to Lourdes, whose birth had realigned her thinking. It's one of the most touching songs on the LP, and also has perhaps the oddest provenance of all the songs on the album (odder even than 'Shanti/Ashtangi', a Sanskrit poem for which she required pronunciation lessons from Indian linguist Vagish Shastri). It's the only track on the album co-credited to an outside composer, in this case the American poet Rod McKuen. His name is on it because it used a sample from a recording of one of his poems, 'Why I Follow the Tigers'. However, the sample is just a second long, consisting of a male voice intoning a few words, which doesn't immediately explain why McKuen is credited as co-author. The reason is that, although it was the only part of his poem actually used, 'Drowned World' had the same general storyline as his work. He explained at the time, "'Drowned' follows the plot line of Tigers, which is why Anita and I receive co-author credit on the song and not merely sampling mention."

It's a tricky call. Madonna had come across 'Why I Follow the Tigers' on a 1969 album called *For Lovers*, an easy-listening collection recorded by the San Sebastian Strings. McKuen and the aforesaid Anita Kerr were the main force behind the Strings, with McKuen writing their lyrics and Kerr the music. (Between 1967 and 1975, they produced a dozen San Sebastian albums, which are now collectors' items.) The poem does have roughly the same theme as Madonna's song – the idea of searching for fulfilment by throwing oneself into frantic activity, only to end up more alone. However, 'Drowned World' doesn't duplicate any of McKuen's lines – but perhaps Madonna decided the thematic similarity was enough to warrant a co-writing credit. Not surprisingly, McKuen was happy with the outcome, writing, "I think Madonna's lyric is terrific (and by the way, so are the royalties generated by the track)."

It would also be interesting to know what led her to use the McKuen sample in the first place. There seems to be no musical affinity – the dreamy mood-music style of 'Why I Follow the Tigers' was the diametrical opposite of her own leanings. It could be a case of nostalgia: McKuen was the most popular American poet of the late 60s – a kind of people's bard, whose books were best-sellers despite critical derision – and it's likely that Madonna had encountered his work when she was growing up. Thus, she may have been drawn to the poem through a combination of childhood memories and an appreciation of its gentle folksiness. (Contrastingly, English writer

Max Blagg received payment but no author credit for the use of one of his poems in the track 'Sky Fits Heaven'. The song incorporates two full lines from Blagg's 'What Fits', which had become famous after he read it aloud in a 1992 Gap TV ad, but he and Madonna struck an agreement whereby he got a fee but no mention in the credits.)

There was also a claim, presumably facetious, from Magnetic Poetry, the company that manufactures tiny magnetic tiles with words printed on them. It contended that Madonna had composed the song 'Candy Perfume Girl' using their kit – apparently, nearly every word in the track matched a word on a tile. This only holds water in the sense that the song lyric is full of nouns stuck together in apparently random order (such as...well... "candy", "perfume" and "girl"), and one could almost imagine Madonna rummaging through tiles and using words that appealed to her. In any case, she denied ever having heard of Magnetic Poetry - but even if she had, it seems a bit much for the company to suggest that its product was responsible for the way the lyric was written.)

'Drowned World' was a guidepost to the rest of the album: egotism and fleshly appetites were out; personal growth and compassion were in. A quote from a 2005 interview with Geordie Greig of the *Sunday Times* is relevant here. Although it pertains to the failure of her marriage to Sean Penn, it could just as well apply to most of her life before *Ray of Light*: "I was completely obsessed with my career, and not ready to be generous in any shape or form."

By the time of the 2005 interview, she'd acquired the wisdom to see how she might have done things differently, but in 1998 – a new mother and a new religious acolyte - she was only just developing that sort of perspective. Previously, she'd prided herself on her toughness – in an interview in the October 1996 issue of American *Vogue,* she said, "If what I've gone through hasn't killed me yet, nothing's going to. That's my opinion."

But by 1998, she was beginning to regret her "obsession", and *Ray of Light* was her great leap away from the things that once consumed her. She's never looked back – every subsequent album has continued her personal-growth journey, consequently breeding an interest in political activism and social commentary. (On the 2002 album *American Life,* she incorporated her thoughts about the state of the nation into the music, with mixed artistic results.)

As with all of her albums, her state of mind is reflected in the cover art. *Ray of Light*'s is a startling departure. Shot by Mario Testino, another fashion-photographer friend, it presents her as an ethereal goddess, giving the camera a sidelong glance as a breeze wafts through her honey-blonde curls. Her makeup is minimal (though self-tan seems to have been applied – another point of difference from previous sleeves, where alabaster skin was a feature), and her light-reflecting jacket is a watercolour-blue, adding to the impression that she's floating in space. Most striking, though, is her expression. Her gaze is cool and equivocal – a Mona Lisa pose that reveals nothing of her thoughts.

Inside the booklet are shots of her singing – head thrown back, mouth wide, hair frothing around her face. A nipple is visible under her top – for old times' sake, perhaps - but in every other respect the photos unveil a transformation. "Soul-searching" comes to mind: the impression is of a woman in search of serenity. What she's escaping from is depicted in the video for the album's title track, a speeded-up clip of frantic urban isolation – people racing through the streets, galloping through meals and living on top of each other but never connecting. (The Jonas Akerlund-directed clip was voted Video of the Year by VH1 viewers.)

Her quest for enlightenment fills the album, track after track. She fearlessly espouses unfashionable ideas, such as the notion – beloved of 1960s hippies – of finding oneself by going to India. 'Shanti/Ashtangi', a "yoga poem" adapted from a longer text called 'Yoga Taravali', has her chanting in Sanskrit, conjuring up visions of the Beatles in their Maharishi period. Only Orbit's techno-rave soundbed reminds us that it's the late '90s.

She revealed a New Agey approach to spirituality that was very much of its time. Her religious studies, which included Hinduism, Kabbalah and Buddhism, as well as the Catholicism on which she'd been brought up, had led her to believe that all faiths were interconnected. Of everything she had tried, yoga came most naturally, and with 'Shanti/Ashtangi' (and also 'Sky Fits Heaven') she was paying homage to her new value system.

Yoga had become a mainstay. Though she originally took it up because, after giving birth by Caesarean, she needed a low-impact fitness routine, she found herself responding to its philosophy of uplifting the spirit by letting go of desire. Once she began to study it seriously, she professed to finding Paramahansa Yogananda's 1946 guidebook, *Autobiography of a Yogi,* more beneficial than seeing her therapist.

It was ironic, then, that she roused the wrath of a Hindu organization shortly after the record was released. Performing 'Shanti/Ashtangi' and the track 'Ray of Light' at that year's MTV awards, she wore a henna "Vaishnava tilak" facial marking and a tight white vest top

Above Far Left: Note the red Kabbalah bracelet – a symbol of her dedication to the esoteric form of Judaism.

Above: Madonna performing at the VH1 Fashion Awards at Madison Square Garden in New York City.

that outlined her bosom, a combination deemed culturally insensitive by the California-based World Vaishnava Association.

The group, which represented followers of the Vaishnava branch of Hinduism, issued an angry statement: "Madonna's MTV stage performance, which combined Eastern mysticism with Western hedonism, did not sit well with sincere Hindus, Vaishnavas and yoga practitioners around the globe. By wearing this sacred marking while wearing clothing through which her nipples were clearly visible and while gyrating in a sexually suggestive manner with her guitar player, Madonna offended Hindus and Vaishnavas throughout the world."

Madonna's publicist, Liz Rosenberg, told New York's *Daily News* (which covered the row under the memorable headline "Madonna's Bad Karma Stirs Hindu Hullaballoo") that the singer was "very surprised", as she hadn't intended to offend. Rosenberg added dryly, "Why don't they pick on Gwen Stefani [the No Doubt singer, who also used the tilak markings]?" A few days later, Madonna released a tart rejoinder: "The essence of purity and divinity is non-judgement... they should practice what they preach... if they're so pure, why are they watching MTV?"

Many celebrities before her had taken a similarly meandering path to self-discovery (and many more would follow in her footsteps after she turned Kabbalah into the go-to faith for questing superstars), so there was nothing new about her conversion from the material to the ethereal. And if yoga had helped her on the road to inner peace, then there is much to be said for it. Yet it's mildly dispiriting to see her turn into the equivalent of a gap-year student who's gone travelling and discovered that we're all brothers and sisters underneath. One had expected more rigour.

Rigour was instead reserved for bringing up her kids. Famously, she didn't allow Lourdes, her brother Rocco or her adopted children, David and Mercy, to watch TV, which she termed "the poison box": "I'm trying to stimulate them to think for themselves," she revealed to *Q* magazine's Paul Rees in 2002. "We give them books to read instead."

Lourdes had inspired several *Ray of Light* songs: not just 'Drowned World', but 'Sky Fits Heaven' and 'Little Star', all of them attesting to the euphoria of motherhood. The closing track, 'Mer Girl', was about a different mother-daughter relationship: Madonna's with her own mother. It's one of her most naked songs, and certainly her spookiest. She writes of her desire to run away from both her daughter and from the memory of her mother – the grandmother Lourdes would never know – but, mostly, it's a ghostly memoir of her mother's death. Backed by a barely-there synth drone, she sings quietly and affectingly of her five-year-old self's reaction

to her mother's illness, and her horror at her physical disintegration. It's unlike anything else on the record, or in the rest of her catalogue for that matter, and closes the album on a distinctly unsettling note.

If 'Drowned World' and 'Mer Girl' are the album's cathartic bookends, the chunk in between is where she sets out her stall. The techno wig-out title track, the classically inflected 'Frozen', the electronica ballad 'The Power of Good-bye': they're the revelations of a woman approaching 40 who has seen the light.

Amid all this, Orbit's electronic textures, comprised of trance, house and ambient, are the album's ace in the hole: without their futuristic (and danceable) sheen, it's hard to imagine the songs having the impact they do. Yet the emotion in Madonna's voice – much stronger since singing lessons expanded her range – gives Orbit's tracks the human touch they would otherwise lack. Her vocals, in fact, are another of *Ray of Light*'s core strengths – not simply because she's no longer restricted to one high-pitched register but because the lessons unlocked a shimmering lower range that worked beautifully with Orbit's effects. Between voice and effects, the pair came up with an album that simulates the feeling of floating.

"She's steering a brave new course," said *USA Today*'s Edna Gundersen. On the album's 15th anniversary, in 2013, Idolator's Stephen Sears found it had stood the test of time: "...an album light years ahead of its predecessors in scope and musicality."

> "I was
> completely
> obsessed with
> my career,
> and not
> ready to be
> generous in
> any shape
> or form."
>
> *Madonna*

Above Left: Showing the extent to which she was inspired by Eastern cultures, Madonna performs in a sari at the 1998 MTV Video Music Awards.

Right: A relaxed Madonna poses backstage at the BBC TV studios, London in 1998. *Ray of Light* is credited with bringing techno and electronica into the mainstream.

"It's a great feeling to be powerful."

Madonna

A few reviewers were also disappointed that Orbit's sonics hadn't been more experimental, sniping that he wasn't up to the task of producing a truly cutting-edge electronic album. But what she'd been after was something softer; before meeting Orbit, she'd been listening to trance and trip-hop, and his hazy, sensual style fit her idea of how she wanted the record to sound.

Commercially, *Ray of Light* was her biggest success in 10 years. After the disappointments of *Erotica* and *Bedtime Stories*, she was restored to her position as one of the top-selling artists in the world; the record eventually sold 20 million copies, and is the third biggest LP of her career. When awards season came round, she went home with a dozen major ones: four Grammys, including Best Pop Album; a remarkable six from MTV, including the night's top prize, Video of the Year (for the single 'Ray of Light'); three from the American Society of Composers, Authors and Publishers. Attesting to her global popularity, there were plenty of accolades from outside North America, including the delightfully-titled Golden Giraffe Award from the Hungarian music industry.

What *Ray of Light* lacked was a Number 1 American single ('Frozen', the first track released from it, did reach the top in Britain). Of the four tracks released in the United States, 'Frozen' was the biggest hit, reaching Number 2, but 'Ray of Light', 'The Power of Good-bye' and 'Nothing Really Matters' told a story of diminishing returns, each charting lower than the last – at 5, 11 and 93, respectively.

That Number 93 still stands as her lowest ever chart position, apart from a handful of singles released in the 2000s that would miss the chart altogether. American fans maintained that the song was released too late, after radio play had peaked; some claimed it hadn't had enough radio exposure in the first place. (Lack of airplay would become an issue for some fans as the 2000s progressed; in 2006, when the track 'Sorry' stalled at Number 58, 3,000 people signed a petition titled End the Madonna on US Radio Boycott.)

Yet, overall, *Ray of Light* was a triumph: proof that Madonna was still potent as a symbol and an artist.

Despite the near-universal love, it must be added that more than a few critics rolled their eyes at the idea of a superstar turning to New Age balm to ease her midlife crisis. The feminist commentator Suzanne Moore, a staunch fan, took aim at these critics in a supportive piece in the *Independent* the week after *Ray of Light*'s release. "Is all this going with the New Age flow any deeper, any more meaningful than [*Absolutely Fabulous* character] Edina Monsoon's chanting and crystal healing?" she asked, summing up the tone of some reviews.

Springing to her defence, Moore maintained that Madonna's Catholic upbringing had given her a lifelong connection to mysticism, rendering her interest in Kabbalah and yoga legitimate and meaningful. But mainly, Moore added, she was admirable for refusing to seek approval, ever. An old rock band cliché comes to mind: "We just do what we do, and if anybody else likes it, that's a bonus." That – as Moore might have said – sums up Madonna's entire career: she does what she does, and whether the public approve or disapprove is immaterial.

But even here, provoking Edina comparisons, Madonna was ahead of the zeitgeist. The 1980s Me Generation was now entering middle age; having sated their appetite for physical possessions, many were searching for a meaning beyond materialism. Madonna, bellwether of the Me's, was providing an answer.

Above and Right: Madonna as a geisha (albeit one dressed by Gaultier) in the 'Nothing Really Matters' video. To date, the song has never been performed on any of Madonna's concert tours.

CHAPTER 9
MUSIC

Music *took Madonna back to the dance floor, in the company of futuristic electronica producer Mirwais Ahmadzaï. Though still spiritual in tone (and sometimes bonkers – Madonna goes alt-country!), this was a summons to dance.*

At MTV's European Music Awards, where she received two gongs. Stockholm, November 2000.

MUSIC

Working with "a French guy called Mirwais", Madonna
soft-pedals the spirituality and returns to the dancefloor.
There's a new baby, a wedding and a starring role in a film
directed by her new husband – but it's really all about the Music.

There she is on the back cover of *Music*, a woman in cowboy hat and blue-satin rodeo shirt, peering with great interest at the acoustic guitar she was holding. Madonna? A cowgirl? With a guitar? Yet the contents of her eighth studio album were anything but homespun. She had introduced a new producer to the fold – the Paris-based Mirwais Ahmadzaï, who made his reputation in progressive dance music – but had also retained William Orbit, resulting in an album full of sparkling, straight-up dance tracks.

She began work on it in September 1999; by the time it appeared, 12 months later, she was a mother of two. She had met English filmmaker Guy Ritchie in 1998, at a party given by Sting's wife, Trudie Styler. Ritchie was then one of the rising stars of Brit-cinema, and Styler had been executive producer on his debut gangster caper, *Lock, Stock and Two Smoking Barrels*, which was viewed as the start of a promising directing career. Just 29 when it came out, he was a whole new variety of love interest for Madonna.

Most of her swains since Sean Penn had been eclipsed by her fame, but Ritchie had a high-profile career of his own. Additionally, he was English, which endowed him with a pleasant exoticism. She'd dated Brits before (most notably an actor called Andy Bird, who claimed their relationship was ruined by incessant press intrusion), and had

worked with William "Billy Bubbles" Orbit, but Ritchie was in effect her official introduction to British manhood.

Most importantly, he was undaunted by the baggage that came with dating a household name. Many men, she'd complained in the past, were too intimidated to go out with her, but Ritchie was cut from a different cloth. His comfortable upbringing undoubtedly helped, but he wasn't short of confidence, and had an irreverent streak that she loved – at least initially. He was responsible for the name "Madge", which was seized on delightedly by the UK media. In Britain, she remains Madge to this day.

She took the nickname in good humour at first, but came to resent it – possibly because she didn't understand it. In a 2009 chat with David Letterman, she said, "Some people say Madge is a colloquialism for a boring, middle-aged housewife and some people say it's short for 'Majesty'." Well...maybe. But there's also another explanation, which has nothing to do with housewives. There was Ritchie, a 29-year-old wooing a vastly rich cultural symbol who also happened to be 10 years older than him. The playing field needed to be levelled if the relationship was to succeed. The

Right: A far cry from *Music*'s cowgirl image: at the Sutton Place Hotel, Toronto, February 2000.

"It is a gift for her to have recorded 'American Pie'. I think her version is sensual and mystical."

Don McLean

best way was to subvert the name "Madonna" and the iconography that went with it. As "Madonna" she was a star; as "Madge", the girl next door. It was a quintessentially Brit way of poking fun at power, but it seems she didn't quite get it. "That's one of the reasons I left England, so I don't have to hear the word 'Madge' any more," she said to Letterman.

To be fair, once she began spending more time in the UK as the relationship developed, she worked hard at assimilating. She was a keen student of things English, learning to ride and adopting the Anglicisms Ritchie taught her. Her interviews were soon speckled with Brit vernacular; she told one interviewer he was "talking bollocks", and another that she'd developed a fondness for "a half of a pint" of Timothy Taylor Landlord ale. (After a snifter of Timothy Taylor, she confided during a BBC interview, "I become one of those English drunken girls," which suggested she had yet to meet any proper English drunken girls.)

Most famously, she revealed to Radio 1 DJ Jo Whiley in 2001 that Ritchie didn't like her to show her "raspberries" in public – "raspberries" supposedly translating as "nipples". The comment was mocked by those who thought it a bit rich that the upper-crust Ritchie used Cockney rhyming slang – even more so, that Midwestern gal Madonna had adopted it. Happily, Ritchie's edict didn't change her behaviour much, and she never lost her Americanness, despite a brief period when she developed an English-ish accent.

She gave birth to their son, Rocco John, on August 11, 2000, and the couple married on December 22 of that year at a ceremony at Skibo Castle in the Scottish Highlands. Security at the wedding – attended by a host of high-profile friends, including Stella McCartney (who made the wedding dress) and Gwyneth Paltrow – was so tight that it was years before any photos emerged. In 2008, a British tabloid published 10 pictures that had been copied surreptitiously by one of Madonna's employees, the first time shots of the wedding had been published anywhere in the world. She and Ritchie sued for breach of privacy and copyright infringement, and in 2009 won substantial damages (which were donated to her charity Raising Malawi).

Thus, by the time *Music* appeared, a month after Rocco's birth, she was happily settled, with a new baby and about to be married. Curiously, none of this homeliness is evident from its sound. *Music* is a record based on inorganic shards of sound: Auto-Tune, warped beats

and the kind of metallic disco pioneered by Daft Punk. It was also the first Madonna album not to have the lyrics, apart from the title track, printed on the sleeve. The inference is that she was feeling less introspective this time, that the important thing now was the beats.

For those who wanted the lyrics, the sleeve advised that they were available on her website – a sign of the internet's increasing importance in her relationship with fans. She was an enthusiastic adopter of technology, having used it to address her public since the era of *Bedtime Stories*. Perceiving that it wasn't just effective but also safe – providing a barrier between herself and overly enthusiastic admirers – she increasingly incorporated it into promotional activities. Two months after *Music*'s release, she staged two of the first-ever internet gigs – a two-in-one promo masterstroke that broadcast her to a huge audience while also sending the message that she was au fait with technology.

(That said, she had been decidedly displeased when the title song leaked online via Napster in May 2000, three months before it was due to be released as a single. Unauthorized file-sharing was about to explode into a huge industry issue due to a lawsuit filed by metal band Metallica against Napster only a month before. Madonna had the foresight to realize that file-sharing would generate a culture in which people expected to get music for free, and she tartly announced that she had no intention of giving her work away.)

The LP artwork features the words to the track 'Music' superimposed on more cowgirl photos. In the centrefold, she's asleep on a bale of hay, a thoroughly American image that contrasts with the Euro-techno sound inside. In an online chat with fans on AOL just after the album appeared, she acknowledged the "irony" of dressing like a rodeo princess for an album constructed with synthesizers. The clothes, she said, were a way of being in harmony with nature and her US roots, and she relished the incongruity of the look versus the sound within.

On the record, there's a nod to those roots: an Americana number called 'Don't Tell Me', her first-ever attempt at country music. The simplest and most mainstream song on the album, it even features acoustic guitar and was co-written by folk-blues singer Joe Henry, who's

Right: Madonna in 2000, just months after giving birth to Rocco, her son with Guy Ritchie.

married to her sister, Melanie. (Henry's own rootsy version of the song, titled 'Stop', is also worth hearing.) Released as *Music*'s second single, it became a smash, reportedly selling 4 million copies worldwide. It's easy to see why: ranking among her prettiest ballads, this is an understated love song (or is it? The lyric is deeply ambiguous; she could be renewing a vow of love, or just as easily pushing someone away).

Music contains one other anomaly: a cover of Don McLean's ruminative 1971 hit 'American Pie'. It's included on the European version only; in the US, it appears on the soundtrack album to the 2000 film *The Next Best Thing*, in which she starred with Rupert Everett. (The picture got scathing notices, and won Madonna another Razzie for her role as a straight woman who had a baby with her gay male friend.) Madonna has a magic touch when it comes to soundtrack songs – nearly every one released as a single has achieved a high chart placing, and 'American Pie' maintained the tradition.

Despite some negative reviews (her vocal, claimed the *NME*, had "all the impact of a step-class instructor with a hopeless crush on the fat one out of Westlife"), the song reached Number 1 in many countries, including Britain. McLean himself was a fan of her interpretation, saying, "It is a gift for her to have recorded 'American Pie'. I think [her version] is sensual and mystical."

When heard alongside the other songs on *Music*, however, its deficiencies are obvious. It's not as lacklustre as "step-class instructor"

makes it sound (and which member of Westlife was that, by the way?), but Madonna sounds detached, as if she'd phoned in her vocals. The whole thing makes considerably more sense as a video. This shows a succession of ordinary Americans, mainly in couples, some of them same-sex; two women are seen kissing (though this was cut from the version aired on MTV). In this context, the detachment in her vocals can be viewed as deliberate; she's allowing the people in the video to take centre stage, rather than be upstaged by her.

'American Pie' was her first hit of the new century, which demands that we briefly mention her last hit of the old one. It was another soundtrack number, this time from *Austin Powers: The Spy Who Shagged Me*. Titled 'Beautiful Stranger', it was specifically written for the film, and the video even had Madonna flirtatiously "interacting" with Austin. The last 20 seconds of the video, in which she and Austin are driving back to his pad in the mutual expectation of good loving, is arguably her funniest screen scene ever. Yet the song wasn't the lightweight throwaway one might have expected. It was a reverb-laden psychedelic number that fit somewhere between Love's 1966 single 'She Comes in Colors' and Siouxsie and the Banshees' cover of the Beatles' 'Dear Prudence' – and it struck a chord in Britain, where it got 2,462 radio plays in one week, the most then ever recorded for any single.

Having dispatched 'American Pie' and 'Beautiful Stranger', Madonna got on with putting together *Music*. She announced on her website that she was working with "a French guy called Mirwais and he is the shit". As it happened, she really did think he was "the shit". She'd been introduced to him by her Maverick business partner, Guy Oseary, who was thinking of signing the half-Afghan/half-Italian producer as an artist. When she heard his demo, it was a thunderbolt moment. Having been considering where to go from *Ray of Light*'s ambient sound, she'd found the answer.

"Have you ever met Mirwais?" she asked the British journalist Simon Garfield in an interview in the *Observer* several years later. "Jean-Paul Sartre comes to mind. He's very intellectual, very analytical, very cerebral, very existential, very philosophical." In other words, he was unlike anyone she had worked with before, and in particular a complete contrast to the cheerful Orbit. Mirwais' career stretched

Left: A still from the 'American Pie' video, which showed a procession of ordinary Americans, including same-sex couples.

Above: Sisterly solidarity: bigging up Kylie Minogue in a customized T-shirt at the MTV Europe Awards in 2000.

back to the early 80s in France, when he'd been the guitarist in an art-punk band called Taxi Girl. He came late to dance music, but by the late 90s he was making futuristic electronica.

His big solo hit was a squelchy 1998 track called 'Disco Science', which was one of the tracks he'd sent to Oseary. Its bleeps, whooshes and slow-building release prefigured the sound he would develop for Madonna. Essentially, its clean minimalism was the opposite of her trance-oriented work with Orbit, chiming with her policy of never repeating herself. She described the difference between *Ray of Light* and *Music* two months after *Music*'s release. *Ray of Light*, she explained, was marked by trippiness and a dense, ambient texture. *Music*, on the other hand, was sparser, simpler and funkier. By that point it had sold 4 million copies.

Back in 1999, when she had first heard Mirwais' demo, she "flipped over it", instantly realizing what he'd be able to do. She asked Oseary to see if the producer would fancy working with her. "I was surprised but not scared when she called," Mirwais told *The Face* in April 2000. "She really understands music. She taught me about simplicity."

At first, working together was not easy. His English was patchy, and she spoke little French (though she would learn enough to sing part of the song 'Paradise (Not for Me)' in French). His manager had to translate for the first few weeks. The frustration was immense, but – and this is a prime example of Madonna making something happen simply by willing it – once they felt comfortable with each other, his English improved markedly.

He persuaded her not to use any effects on her voice, other than on a few tracks like 'Music' and 'Nobody's Perfect', where a vocoder distorts her pitch. Otherwise, her vocals are unadulterated and raw, which, for a pop singer, is tantamount to stripping naked. In another departure, she recorded most of it in London; the first time she'd ever made an album outside America. In 2000, the UK was leagues ahead of the US, as far as electronic music went; the American charts were dominated by hip hop and boy bands like N Sync, while the UK was well into its second decade of producing the kind of club stormers she wanted to emulate.

So would America appreciate what she was doing? The album had few reference points that US audiences would understand. All its producers

CHAPTER 10
AMERICAN LIFE

Madonna gets political; fans flee. Or so it seemed: the clubby, spiky American Life made clear her feelings about where her country was heading, to widespread lack of love from the public. Its 5 million sales are among the lowest of any of her albums.

American Life was Madonna's most political album to date. It received mixed reviews and was her first album not to produce a US hit single.

AMERICAN LIFE

On the most caustic album of her career, Madonna takes aim at celebrity culture and the war in Iraq. There's a new freedom-fighter image, and a video so contentious that she withdraws it. But there's also a kiss with Britney Spears to be going on with.

It was "underwhelming", said the *Guardian*'s Alexis Petridis. "Misconceived" was the judgment of the *Village Voice*'s Jessica Winter, while *Stylus* magazine's Ed Howard asked, feelingly, "Where, exactly, did Madonna start to go wrong?"

Although *American Life* also picked up positive reviews (indeed, every reviewer above also found things to enjoy, with Petridis even declaring, *"American Life*'s best tracks make a mockery of virtually all other current pop music"), this was the first time in Madonna's career that a release had provoked such disappointment. For a novel reason, too – this time, she was being slated not for being a threat to society, but for not being threatening enough. When had she ever been accused of being "underwhelming"? And Mirwais, who produced nearly the entire album, came in for a drubbing for falling back on the chopped-and-diced sound he'd used on *Music*.

The public evidently agreed with the reviewers, and failed to buy it in their millions. In America, it was her first album not to produce a hit single: the title track clambered to Number 37, but the next three singles all failed even to enter the Top 100. The UK, as usual, was more receptive, and of the four singles released, three reached the Top 20. Eleven years on, worldwide sales stand at around 5 million, making it the lowest-selling of her first nine albums.

The problem, it seemed, was that it was a record of mixed messages, none of them immediately alluring. On the cover, she mimicked the famous photo of Che Guevara that had been on the wall of every 1970s college student. She even wore the beret and used the photo-negative effect – though she was staring directly into the lens, with an expression that could be read as "What are you looking at, punk?" Inside the booklet, she posed in a military-style jumpsuit (and high heels), holding an assault rifle, evoking the notorious 1974 picture of the heiress-turned-bank-robber Patty Hearst.

The confrontational approach carried over into the music itself. To toughen her sound, she made her first serious attempt at rapping (MC Madge's efforts are heard on several tracks, including 'American Life'). And if that did not by itself prove that she had serious things to convey, there was a deliberate paucity of *Music*-style escapism in the lyrics. The three songs opening *American Life* (the title track, 'Hollywood' and 'I'm So Stupid') set the abrasive tone for much of the LP. These were anything but hands-in-the-air party tunes. Instead, they were intended to be satirical takedowns of celebrity culture. In

Right: Madonna at the Manhattan launch party for her friend Rabbi Yehuda Berg's book, *The 72 Names of God.*

a VH1 special aired in April 2003, a few days before the LP came out, she made it clear that she wasn't in the mood for partying. Rather, she wanted "to shout from the rooftops that we have all been living in a dream...and we have to wake up to reality".

The critical response was withering. Much of the slating was aimed at those three opening tracks, which were written from the viewpoint of a showbiz insider who's finally decided that money and adulation are a load of hooey. It's true that she'd already covered some of this territory on *Ray of Light*, but that album was more a therapy session and her observations were directed at herself. This time she was preaching to the world – and the world tends to be irritated by privileged people taking it upon themselves to announce that everyone else has got it wrong.

You could almost see the *Guardian*'s Petridis rolling his eyes as he wrote, "It turns out...that money can't buy you happiness and that fame isn't all it's cracked up to be." AVClub.com denounced the title track as "...jittery, tuneless and shallow to the point of self-parody". Even more cuttingly, the song came ninth in a *Blender* magazine list titled The 50 Worst Songs Ever, sandwiched between the Paul McCartney/ Stevie Wonder hit 'Ebony and Ivory' and Eddie Murphy's 'Party All the Time'. "The song – propelled by a constipated digital beat and some bungled musings on celebrity culture – stinks the whole way through," pronounced *Blender*.

And then there was the 'American Life' video.

A discussion of it must be prefaced by a reminder that both the album and its first single appeared in April 2003, midway through the American invasion of Iraq; the video came out a few weeks earlier. This timing was coincidental; album releases are planned too far in advance for events to have been foreseen. But the caustic tone of the music, and the LP sleeve, were taken by many as a pronouncement on the state of American democracy. Certainly, her "living in a dream" comments could be interpreted as addressing both the Western world's fascination with celebrities and the actions of the American government since 9/11.

Right: Britney Spears, Madonna and Christina Aguilera at the 2003 MTV Video Music Awards. The performance would include Madonna and Spears' infamous kiss.

"We have all been living in a dream... and we have to wake up to reality."

Madonna

In that VH1 interview, she expressed disquiet about America trying to impose "democracy" on Iraq when the democratic rights of Americans themselves were being violated by the Bush administration. Anyone who'd publicly protested against the invasion had been "punished", she said, and she was alarmed at the erosion of Constitutional rights.

Into this heated atmosphere came 'American Life'. The single in itself wasn't especially contentious, being little more than a moan about the emptiness of the entertainment world. The video, however, was contentious – and then some. Indeed, it seemed designed to induce apoplexy in those of a right-wing bent. Its only thematic connection with the song it was promoting was that its setting was a fashion show – fashion being one of the superficial industries condemned in the song. But this fashion show was a different sort of event. The models were dressed in combat fatigues and gas masks, and the video screens behind them showed missiles leaving their silos, and explosions. Two models wore Islamic hijabs and robes, and a young Middle Eastern boy sauntered down the catwalk with a bullet belt slung around his neck.

This was all observed by the usual fashion-show audience of beautiful hipsters, who registered no emotion – not even when Madonna, decked out as American military top brass, led a troupe of combat-ready women in a catwalk invasion. (She drove onto the runway in a Mini Cooper, which was name-checked in the lyric; piquantly, toy versions of the Mini were given to the British press as a promotional item.) The clip ends with a George Bush lookalike lighting his cigar with a hand grenade.

Subtle, this wasn't. Just before release, her label released an explanatory statement: "[It] expresses a panoramic view of our culture and looming war through the view of a female superhero portrayed by Madonna. Starting as a runway show of couture army fatigues, the fashion show escalates into a mad frenzy depicting the catastrophic repercussions and horrors of war." The grenade sequence, according to Madonna herself, showed a weapon being transformed into "something that is completely innocuous".

But soon she realized that she'd misjudged the tenor of public feeling. She may have been spooked by the fury aroused by the country trio Dixie Chicks, who made what was considered an inflammatory remark at a London gig in March. The comment hardly seems inflammatory now

("Just so you know, we're on the good side with y'all. We do not want this war, this violence, and we're ashamed that the President of the United States is from Texas"), but it unleashed a furious backlash in America. Fans boycotted their records and a corporate sponsor dropped them, which showed the strength of feeling among conservatives. On April 1, on the eve of the video's premiere, Madonna withdrew it, explaining, "Due to the volatile state of the world and out of sensitivity and respect to the armed forces, who I support and pray for, I do not want to risk offending anyone who might misinterpret the meaning of this video."

To replace it, she hastily filmed a clip of her singing – still dressed in military gear – in front of a succession of international flags. It was conciliatory yet pointed: Madonna may have been forced to jettison the more extreme version, but her peace-and-brotherhood message was still loud and clear.

In 2013, a fansite called Guy Penn and the Gospel According to Madge reflected that the video had been "an accurate foretelling of the past decade", but at the same time had "marked the demise of Madonna the American radio star." There is something to that, inasmuch as she's had only three Top 10 US singles in the eleven years since – and of these, two ('4 Minutes' and 'Give Me All Your Luvin'') were undoubtedly helped along by the presence of guest stars Justin Timberlake, Timbaland, Nicki Minaj and MIA. That said, she remains a force in the *Billboard* Hot Dance Club chart, compiled by nightclub DJs; nearly every single she's put out since 'American Life' has reached the top of that chart, and she holds the record for most Number 1s on it: 43.

One wonders what would have happened had she not pulled the video, which remains the only moment of self-censorship in her career. It's likely that the above-mentioned volatility would have generated a Dixie Chicks-style boycott or unofficial airplay ban, which would have also affected future releases. Withdrawing it was the sensible thing to do – and the fall-off in hit singles was always on the cards anyway. Some fans have maintained that the singles she's put out in the last few years would have fared better with more promotion, but that's probably wishful thinking: the pop industry prioritizes young artists, while the veterans find that singles sales dry up. (One of the few exceptions is Tina Turner, who had a remarkable second blossoming in the pop charts in her mid-40s, turning out half a dozen major hits in the mid-1980s).

As ever, the power lies with record-buyers, and in the case of *American Life*, they found her stern new reinvention unpalatable. Though it hit Number 1 in the US chart, it had sold just 680,000 copies there by 2012.

Left: Madonna performing songs from *American Life* at the MTV studios, New York, April 2003.

Above: Her spikiest album, *American Life* unsparingly examined her relationship with fame and Hollywood.

"I'm not saying those girls can't grow into something, but...everything's so homogenized."

Madonna

To put this in context: in 2003, the year of its release, the five biggest-selling albums in the world were Norah Jones' *Come Away with Me*, Avril Lavigne's *Let Go*, Shania Twain's *Up!*, 50 Cent's *Get Rich or Die Tryin'* and Christina Aguilera's *Stripped*, which illustrates how little appetite there was for an album of sombre political opinion-mongering, even if there was little actual politics in the songs.

More confusingly – returning to the "mixed messages" mentioned earlier in the chapter – other songs were dedicated to her current personal state of domestic bliss. 'Love Profusion', 'Intervention' and 'Nothing Fails', in particular, depicted her as happily in love with husband and family. And the track 'Mother and Father' returned to the well-explored subject of her mother's death and her subsequent anger at her father – though, for the first time, she also showed compassion for him. None of her previous songs on the subject had acknowledged that her father, too, had been devastated, but now she granted him sympathy.

Rounding out the album was 'Die Another Day', the theme from the James Bond film of that name. A stuttering electroclash-house number, it was released months before the album appeared, and had been a hit, reaching the Top 10 and receiving Grammy and Golden Globe nominations (not to mention a Golden Raspberry nomination for Worst Original Song). There was no pressing reason for it to be included on *American Life*, and it feels isolated among the other songs on the record. Still, it did ensure that the LP contained a Top 10 hit.

All told, *American Life* was a complex record that demanded serious engagement, and many weren't willing to meet it halfway. In a reassessment five years after its release, *Slant* magazine decreed it her bravest record, but in the eyes of some it remains the hardest to love.

She began composing the album in late 2001, when the attacks against Washington and New York, including the destruction of the World Trade Center, were fresh in the world's collective consciousness. It was the shock of 9/11 that informed the first songs she wrote: she found herself making an inventory of what was important to her, and re-examining her values. The tracks that became the opening trilogy – 'American Life', 'Hollywood' and 'I'm So Stupid' – represented her view of where Western society had taken a wrong turn. The pursuit of power and the mindless acquisition of "stuff" hadn't made her happy, and hadn't done much for the world, either, she said in early 2003. Thus, by putting those tracks at the start of the record, she was in effect clearing out her cupboards, and leaving the rest of the record for the things that were important to her: home, family and friends.

As she wrote, she was also influenced – in a bemused way – by the advent of TV talent shows such as *Popstars* and *Pop Idol*. Their central tenet – that being famous was an end in itself – wasn't so far removed from her own teenage hunger for recognition, but she was perturbed by the idea that the process was now in the hands of record and TV executives whose aim was to find the most malleable young women and turn them into identical versions of each other. "I'm not saying those girls can't grow into something, but...everything's so homogenized," she told *Q* magazine's Paul Rees.

(Yet she empathized, and struck up a friendship with Britney Spears, who'd started as a Mousketeer and been moulded into a teenage sex symbol. She contributed vocals to Spears' 2003 single 'Me Against the Music', and performed the track 'Hollywood' with her at that year's MTV Video Music Awards. Halfway through the song, she leaned over and gave Britney a seemingly unscripted open-mouthed kiss, which became the ceremony's defining moment and is still famous in the canon of supposedly outrageous VMA moments. Christina Aguilera, also onstage with them, was also kissed, but it's the three-second Britney peck that's remembered.)

After writing a few songs in the autumn of 2001, she took time off to make a movie with Guy Ritchie. As with Sean Penn and *Shanghai Surprise*, the pairing – Ritchie directing Madonna as a rich woman shipwrecked with a sailor – turned out to be a misjudgement. *Swept Away*, an adaptation of a 1974 Lina Wertmuller film, was released in October 2002, and promptly savaged by the press. Critics practically queued to dish out the vitriol, with this sample from John Anderson of *Newsday* epitomizing the general tone: "In fact, new ways of describing badness need to be invented to describe exactly how bad it is."

In America it earned back just under $600,000 of its $10 million budget, while in Britain it was released straight to DVD. Madonna's view was that much of the criticism stemmed from the press wanting to take Ritchie down a peg. He'd been so successful with *Lock, Stock...* and *Snatch*, she said, that the media had decided it was time to knock him down. She was clearly bruised by it. The glowing notices she'd received in *Evita* had seemed to portend a turnaround in her screen fortunes, but the effect hadn't lasted. Her first post-*Evita* movie, the 2000 comedy *The Next Best Thing*, had been slated, and now this – her first major project with her husband – was being treated to the worst reviews she'd had since *Shanghai Surprise*.

There was another foray into acting in 2002: she played an art dealer in the play *Up for Grabs*, which ran for two months in London's West End. Many of the reviews weren't too hard on her performance; the *Guardian*'s Michael Billington decided she wasn't bad, "just technically

awkward", while Philip Fisher acknowledged in *Theatreworld* that, "for so many, the chance to see an iconic superstar on the London stage is far more important than her performance". That was undeniably true: another reviewer devoted several irritated sentences to the behaviour of the fans in the crowd, who apparently spent much of the performance cheering and photographing her, with those in the front row holding their cameras inches from her face.

Back in the studio with Mirwais, she decided on a pared-down approach to the music – a spartan, "under-produced" sound. His trademark – glitchy, stuttering loops that stop and start mid-track, or even in the middle of a word – is all over the music, recalling Kraftwerk. But it's offset by organic elements, such as acoustic guitar and, on 'Hollywood', a sample of early-morning birdsong.

It was also his idea for her to rap at the end of 'American Life' – a little extra that perhaps ought to have been left on the cutting-room floor. She resisted at first, but he persuaded her; having been persuaded, she gave it a good go, freestyling about her everyday life.

Madonna's daily grind is not as others', obviously, so her rap included a list of the people on her staff, from in-house chef to security guards, and concluded with the admission that none of it had made her happy. It was obviously a parody of rich, bored celebrities, but satire often doesn't translate well in pop songs, a point nailed by Andrew Unterberger of PopDust.com in a retrospective review in 2013. The rap, he wrote, "supposedly bemoan[s] the meaningless of it all, but sound[s] more like one long-ass humblebrag".

'Hollywood' and 'Mother and Father' also featured rapping, but they didn't provoke the same degree of bewilderment. Given the subject matter, the rhyming in 'Mother and Father' (delivered in a clipped, Englishy accent) can be taken as a lost-girl playground chant, rather than an attempt to sound "current".

Left: Madonna completed her *American Life* promo tour by performing on British music show *Top of the Pops* in May 2003.

Above: Performing in Inglewood, California in 2004. The outfits for Madonna's Re-Invention Tour were designed by Christian Lacroix.

The album also marked the first time she wrote a song with Stuart Price. An English DJ and producer also known as Jacques Lu Cont and Les Rythmes Digitale, he came to her attention after remixing tracks from *Music*. He was working his way up the Madonna production ladder: after the *Music* remixes, he'd been appointed musical director on her 2001 Drowned World Tour, which led to his co-writing the *American Life* track 'X-Static Process'. Thus primed, he would be given the job of primary producer on her next album, *Confessions on a Dance Floor*.

Her desire to pare down and strip back was also responsible for the sleeve artwork. Partly, the startling sleeve images were a reaction to the pasting she'd taken for *Swept Away*. In the film, she'd been soft and blonde; for *American Life*, she transformed herself into something dark and hard – a warrior. But the new look did more than just salve the sting of *Swept Away*; it also reflected her "revolutionary" state of mind. She considered giving the album a Hebrew name – *Ein Sof* ("the infinite") – which she soon abandoned in favour of the title *Hollywood*, which itself gave way to the final name, *American Life*.

The album came out on April 21, 2003 and sold a highly respectable 241,000 copies in its first week, debuting at Number 1. (The point should be made that, however much pop fashion changes, Madonna's albums are still "event" releases, and every one she's released since *American Life* has reached the top of the charts.) But its four singles – which were the ultimate drivers of album sales, as a string of big singles can keep an LP in the chart for months or years – were unsuccessful. Apart from the title track, which peaked at a disappointing Number 37, none reached the American Top 100. In the UK, the title track and the second single, 'Hollywood', both hit a rather more satisfactory Number 2, but the next song, "Nothing Fails", missed the chart entirely. The fourth release, the pretty, mostly acoustic 'Love Profusion', was a British Number 11.

The following year, she set out on the Re-Invention World Tour, a 56-date behemoth that sold out as soon as tickets went on sale. The name, changed from the original Whore of Babylon World Tour – which would have looked pretty amazing on merchandise – was a gesture of defiance at those who'd questioned her career's-worth of image changes. It was also a statement of intent: she planned to reinvent, retool and repurpose herself for as long as it suited her. Re-Invention was the highest-grossing tour of 2004, confirming that, even if *American Life* hadn't struck a chord, there was still a hunger to see Madonna onstage. In its five segments – French Baroque/Marie Antoinette Revival, Military/Army, Circus/Cabaret, Acoustic and Scottish/Tribal – she confronted her past and future selves, and reaffirmed, if anyone had wondered, that there was nobody else like her.

Above: In combat fatigues, held aloft on a rifle, during the "Military" segment of the Re-Invention Tour.

Right: Madonna performing 'Vogue' during the "French Baroque/Marie Antoinette Revival" segment of the tour.

it was also How She Got Her Groove Back. The album and single restored her groove in a big way, by returning her to the place that always energized her: the dance floor.

The preceding year, 2004, had been given over to the Re-Invention Tour, and to promoting *The English Roses*, a series of children's books she began writing in 2003. Her Kabbalah teacher had been instrumental in the book project, suggesting that she put her spiritual knowledge to use by writing for under-10s. The stories concerned the adventures of a group of young London girls, with each book containing a lightly toasted moral. The first, simply titled *The English Roses*, tackled the subject of jealousy: four girls meet a fifth, who goes by the name Binah (a Hebrew/Kabbalah term meaning "understanding"). She happens to be beautiful, and, naturally, the four are envious, not realizing that Binah is actually lonely and spends her life scrubbing floors and cooking for her widowed father. A fairy godmother arranges for the girls to swap lives with Binah, and they learn a lesson about not judging anyone without knowing them.

Reviewers suggested that there was more than a touch of Madonna's own early life in the story, though she herself said the inspiration for Binah was her own daughter, Lourdes, by now known as Lola. "In school, children can be quite mean, and ostracize her because I'm her mother," she told journalists in September 2003, at a London launch party for the first book. But in the *Observer*, Kate Kellaway was more intrigued "by its aspirational wistfulness, its bid for Englishness".

An interesting supposition, as Madonna was then in the midst of her love affair with England. She and Guy had settled in London, and bought a Wiltshire country estate, which had once been the home of the unimpeachably English Cecil Beaton. Lola and Rocco were enrolled at the Lycée Francais, one of the capital's more prestigious primaries, and their mother threw herself into her new Anglicized life. She learned to ride – which ended in a tumble from a horse in August 2005, limiting the use of her left arm for weeks – and experimented with an English accent ("like Celia Johnson in *Brief Encounter*," according to British journalist Kathryn Flett). And when Bob Geldof asked her to play one of the Live 8 shows in July 2005, she chose the London gig.

Previous Pages & Far Left: Madonna marking the release of *Confessions* with a gig at Koko, London; she had last played there in 1983.

Far Left & Below: Kicking off the MTV Europe awards with the newly released 'Hung Up', which was already a worldwide hit. The single would sell 9 million copies worldwide and was Madonna's 36th Top 10 on the US *Billboard*.

Her enthusiastic adoption of Britishness may have been spawned by having married a Londoner, but her nature drove her to plunge in and carve out her own version of it. Her Englishness was of the upper-crust variety, manifesting itself in the tweedy riding clothes she wore in a photo shoot that appeared in the August 2005 edition of US *Vogue*; it was also there in the Home Counties twang she'd used on the *American Life* track 'Mother and Father'. Guy educated her in country pursuits such as fishing, shooting and appreciating ale: "I could be a connoisseur of ales if I wanted to," she told *Vogue*. That interview also contained an eye-popping description of the party the Ritchies threw at the Wiltshire estate to celebrate their fourth wedding anniversary: they recreated a Beatonian country-house weekend, with each guest performing a party piece on a specially constructed stage. Stella McCartney, Gwyneth Paltrow and Coldplay's Chris Martin sang a spoof song called 'American Wife', Tracey Emin read a poem and Sting played lute.

So it may be that *The English Roses* was part of her campaign to assimilate. At its London launch, she dressed the part of a well-bred young English matron, in a flower-patterned satin dress and chignon. She looked, in fact, like one of the girls in the book's illustrations, which had been beguilingly drawn by Jeffrey Fulvimari. (The series, which spanned a dozen books, was highly successful, with the first three volumes selling a total of 1.5 million copies.)

However, others have claimed that *The English Roses* was more a placeholder to occupy her while she waited for musical inspiration to strike again. This happened during the Re-Invention Tour. Stuart Price was her on-the-road keyboardist and musical director, reprising the role he'd held on the Drowned World Tour, and the pair began to write songs while travelling. His dry humour struck a chord with her, and she found him easy to get on with – more so, at that point, than the cerebral Mirwais, whom she'd earmarked as producer for the follow-up to *American Life*.

When Re-Invention ended, in September 2004, the next immediate project on the agenda was a film, which was to be directed by Luc Besson and star Madonna as an elderly woman looking back on her life. She was also writing its soundtrack, on which she began work as soon as the tour finished. Collaborating (separately) with Mirwais, Price and Pat Leonard, she completed a few songs, one of which was 'Hung

Up'. Then she received the film script from Besson, and found, to her dismay, that she didn't like it. She withdrew from the film, but was so fond of 'Hung Up' that she decided to carry on working with Price, with a view toward making her next album.

He had a home studio in West Kilburn, London – and it really was a "home" studio, consisting of one room in his loft, accessible only by stepladder. It was so small that once he'd installed his mixing desk and keyboards there was space only for a sofa and a kettle. The ceiling was so low he had to stoop, though the 5'4" Madonna managed to stand upright.

When she arrived each morning, coffee in hand, he would already be awake, having not gone to bed the night before. As a DJ, he was used to working all night, and when he sequestered himself in his studio, he forgot about everything else, including eating. Madonna was both amused and appalled by his empty cupboards, and had her staff stock them with food. The rough-and-readiness of it reminded her of her earliest recording sessions, when she and Steve Bray worked in a downtown Manhattan apartment, both so keen to make a record that they didn't mind that the street noises outside were being picked up by the microphones as she sang. Success had isolated her and taken some of the primal joy out of recording an album, but when she was crammed into Price's tiny pad, she reconnected with the excitement of creating music.

She'd already decided that this new record would be a complete departure from the dourness of *American Life*. As she told MTV just before *Confessions* appeared, she'd written *American Life* in a state of agitation, distraught and angry at the state of the world. She'd needed the outlet of that album to express her dismay, and had used it as a political sounding-board. But now she no longer wanted to pontificate; she just wanted, once again, to have fun with music.

She was especially keen to cut loose on the new album because, while preparing to make it, she was also editing a documentary called *I'm Going to Tell You a Secret*, which had been filmed during the Re-Invention

"It turned out to go in the other direction, because the first song resonated so monstrously."

Madonna

Left: The Tokyo show was as much dance performance as gig – Madonna says dance makes her feel "free".

Below: The opening night of the 60-date Confessions tour. The concert was divided into four parts: "Equestrian", "Bedouin", "Glam-Punk" and "Disco".

Right: Just your average Madonna gig – performing 'Live to Tell' wearing a crown of thorns on a mirrored crucifix.

produced an album that was all about freedom and giving in to the moment. Best of all, its prime moments – 'Hung Up', 'Sorry', 'Future Lovers' – were constructed with the same brio and panache as bedrock classics like 'Into the Groove'.

Three more singles were released after 'Hung Up': 'Sorry', 'Get Together' and 'Jump'. All did well in Britain, with 'Sorry' sailing to Number 1 and the others reaching the Top 10. Surprisingly, though, none were hits in America. 'Sorry' reached Number 58, and the other two missed the Top 100 entirely – an unexpected downturn, in light of the sterling chart performance of 'Hung Up'. American fans blamed this on a lack of radio play, and to that end, launched an online petition called End the Madonna on US Radio Boycott . It was dispatched, with around 6,000 signatures, to the CEO of Clear Channel Communications, which owned 1,200 American radio stations.

The petition is still online (signatures have now passed 8,000), and makes rather poignant reading. It says, in part, "The evidence that there is a boycott from American Radio is too obvious for words, as Madonna is currently the leading artist in the world ... Madonna rules the planet, EXCEPT for the USA." It recounts the experiences of frustrated fans who'd phoned major stations to request her songs, and been told they couldn't be added to the playlist until they'd been hits at smaller stations. Some fans, it claimed, had also been told that she was "too old", or didn't fit that particular station's demographic.

By contrast, the petition points out, she was still enduringly popular on MTV – when the petition was written, the videos for 'Hung Up' and 'Sorry' had been the most requested clips on the station's Total Request Live show for days on end. Was she, it speculated, being paid back for expressing opposition to the Iraq war during the *American Life* era?

Clear Channel's response was that *Confessions*' retro feel didn't fit into a Top 40 that was then dominated by hip-hop and R&B. The singles were categorized as "Adult Top 40" rather than "Mainstream 40", meaning that they were less likely to be heard by young people – who are the ones who buy the bulk of singles. Conversely, UK radio continued to love her, for the very reason she couldn't get played on US radio: the prevailing British pop sound was overwhelmingly dance-based, and her nu-disco was a perfect fit. 'Hung Up', 'Sorry' and 'Get Together' were all A-listed at Radio 1, and had the chart success to show for it.

A few years later, America would rediscover dance music (and retitle it EDM, electronic dance music), but it was too late for the *Confessions* singles. A recent comment from a fan on the End the Madonna Boycott petition recognized the irony of it all: "With the shift towards EDM on many stations you all are missing out on an artist that has defined this genre."

And yet... American radio programmers should realize that they dismiss Madonna at their peril. Two years later, she was back in the mainstream Top 3 with the single '4 Minutes'. Not bad for an "Adult Top 40" act.

"*Madonna has changed the way our world sounded, she's changed the way our world looked.*"

Justin Timberlake

the 80s singles in one place conjured up that decade and her predominance in it; owning *The Immaculate Collection* was like owning a chunk of pop-culture history. And, of course, because the songs were unimpeachably brilliant.

Back to 2007: Madonna's deal with Live Nation was reported in the financial section of every paper. This was a 10-year alliance that covered all of her music projects, from albums to touring to merchandise to music-related film and TV ventures, and it would earn her up to $120 million.

Music super-deals had certainly existed before: in 2002, Robbie Williams received a reported £80 million from EMI Records in an arrangement that covered roughly the same territory. But Madonna was breaking new ground by signing with a company that wasn't a traditional record label. She was, in fact, the very first person to sign to Live Nation's Artist Nation wing. "I just feel like it's time to move on and approach music in a different way," she told Jonathon Moran of Australia's *Sunday Telegraph*.

Four years later, in 2011, she signed a three-album agreement with Interscope Records, to run in partnership with the Live Nation deal. Interscope would handle the actual making and distributing of records, while Live Nation oversaw the rest of her music projects. Her tours alone were vastly lucrative: for example, the 2008/09 Sticky & Sweet Tour – an 85-date marathon produced by Live Nation – grossed $408 million, the highest ever for a female artist.

Hard Candy's year of release, 2008, was a turning point in other significant ways. In February, she made her directorial debut with the film *Filth and Wisdom*, which starred Eugene Hütz of the band Gogol Bordello as a musician who funds his art by sexually dominating businessmen. Some reviews were fairly positive, but most critics were, as ever, unimpressed. Though it premiered at the Berlin Film Festival, it ran in cinemas for only six weeks, and did poorly at the American box office. Takings were higher in France and Italy, but its worldwide gross was still only $354,000.

Left: A fun-loving looking Madonna bounces onstage at the 02 Arena, London, in July 2009 on the opening night of the Sticky & Sweet Tour.

In March, she was inducted into the Rock and Roll Hall of Fame in New York. Fellow inductees that night included Leonard Cohen and the Philly-soul pioneers Gamble and Huff. Her presence incited much internet chatter along the lines of "What's she doing there?" – which proved only that some people still didn't get it. In her induction speech, she addressed them directly: "The ones that said I was talentless, that I was chubby, that I couldn't sing, that I was a one-hit wonder – they pushed me to be better, and I am grateful for their resistance."

She was inducted by Justin Timberlake, who neatly captured her significance: "Madonna has changed the way our world sounded, she's changed the way our world looked." Then he added, admirably deadpan, "And somehow she still found time to publicly kiss...someone who I may or may not have kissed myself – while I was in the audience. Of course, you all know who I'm talking about – Sean Penn." Of course, we did all know who he was talking about: his ex-girlfriend, Britney Spears, whose career certainly didn't suffer from it.

In July, Christopher Ciccone published a book with the self-explanatory title *Life with My Sister Madonna*. For many years, her younger brother had been the sibling to whom she was closest, dancing in her early videos and working his way up to artistic director of both the Girlie Show World Tour and the documentary *Truth or Dare*. But they'd drifted apart, and his memoir caused great upset to his sister. According to a subsequent interview with Christopher in the *Evening Standard* in 2012, their relationship gradually improved, to the point where they are again on "perfectly personable" terms.)

Her fiftieth birthday was on August 16, spawning scores of "Madonna at 50" think pieces, most of them warm and congratulatory. Perhaps the most touching was *Vanity Fair*'s career retrospective-cum-celebration, which ended with the prediction that when readers died and arrived in heaven, the DJ would be playing 'Lucky Star'.

But there were also truculent online debates about her place in the great pop scheme of things. One thread, started on a popular forum just before her birthday and titled "Madonna Will be a Bigger Historical Figure Than Elvis or The Beatles", makes entertaining reading. It goes on for eight pages, with fans and non-fans trading increasingly acerbic barbs. For every "Madonna's all about image!", there's someone pointing out that she's released half a dozen albums that are classics of their

Left: Sticky & Sweet was a record-breaker, grossing an incredible $408 million – second only to the Rolling Stones.

Above Right: Madonna arriving at the Berlin screening of her directorial debut, *Filth and Wisdom*, in February 2008.

genre. In one of the more surreal exchanges, someone claims none of her records was as good as Guns N' Roses' *Appetite for Destruction* or AC/DC's *Highway to Hell*, provoking the waspish response, "But you're talking about different genres." The most incisive comment, though, comes from one Torrid Affair, who plaintively says, "People who grew up with Madonna seem to idolize her, not sure why, but they do."

Torrid Affair was right. She was – still is – emblematic of her generation of women, which had now reached middle age. As the Madonna Generation passes each future milestone (sixtieth birthdays, retirement, old age), she'll continue to be seen as their representative, without whom life would have been different – not just for them but for women of all ages. Just as Timberlake said, she "changed the way our world sounded, changed the way our world looked".

Her half-century was also the excuse for scores of tenuously linked articles, including "Madonna Refuses to be 50 – Do You Accept Your Age?", "Madonna Generation of 50-Plus Women Defy Recession" and, perhaps best of all, "Madonna at 50: A Celebrity Hair Retrospective". (Almost as shocking as Madonna reaching 50 was the realization that the original Wannabes were by then in their late thirties, and probably parents themselves. This was the group Torrid Affair meant, the girls and boys whose teenage lives were profoundly shaped by her, just as ineradicably as the Beatles and Elvis influenced their respective generations.)

Among the revelations in her brother's book – most of which were along the lines of "she was a bossy kid" – was his prediction that Madonna and Ritchie's marriage would survive. When he wrote it, they'd been married for seven years, and although Christopher didn't see eye-to-eye with Ritchie he was convinced they were "passionately committed" to staying together. But just three months after the book was published, the couple separated. According to reports, some more sensational than others, there were myriad reasons: Kabbalah; the fact their careers often kept them apart (on the day the split was announced, she was playing a show in Boston and he was in London, working on the film *Sherlock Holmes*); and they'd apparently argued about adopting a baby.

Up to the mid-Noughties, Madonna had talked about wanting more children of their own, but by then the couple were also looking into adoption. In October 2006, she brought home a baby boy called David Banda from Malawi, where she had co-founded Raising Malawi, a charity dedicated to ending child poverty in that country. The adoption – which was touched on in a 2008 anti-poverty documentary she produced, *I Am Because We Are* – was complicated by the fact that Malawian law decreed that adoptive parents needed to be resident there for 18 months. After a legal tussle she'd been allowed to take him to London, and was granted a permanent adoption order in 2008. In 2009, she also adopted a Malawian girl, Chifundo "Mercy" James.

The divorce was finalized in November. Madonna's spokeswoman

told the BBC that Ritchie would receive £50–60 million, including their Wiltshire estate. They agreed to share custody of Rocco and David.

Thus, 2008 was an emotionally challenging year. And into the midst of it came *Hard Candy*, which showed her to be resilient, even bullishly optimistic, about life and love. Admittedly, it was released in March, before her separation and *Life with My Sister*, but even now it still stands as Madonna's definitive reaction to that particular year.

Take the cover photo, which bristles with confidence, much of it emanating from her midriff. That's where she sports a massive, boxing-title belt, engraved with dollar signs and the words Give It To Me and M-Dolla. In the middle of the belt is a huge, rhinestone-studded "M". The last time a belt had been so prominently displayed on one of her sleeves was in 1984; this time around, she's nobody's Boy Toy. The belt is complemented by a knuckle-duster ring with the inscription M-Dolla, a black leotard and black dominatrix-style thigh boots. Just for the sake of continuity, there's a crucifix around her neck.

The word "fierce" comes to mind – a buzzword that's been bandied around a good deal in the last decade or so, mainly to describe female singers who sing at maximum volume while thrashing voluminous

manes of hair and wearing "killer" heels. (Heels are invariably "killer" if the woman wearing them is "fierce".) But those pop stars aren't fierce – not really. This is fierce: a 49-year-old woman wearing exactly what she wants to wear, fixing the camera with her most confrontational stare.

(What we don't see on the cover – though it's captured in the inside photos – is the musculature of her arms, which she had lately honed to sinewy steeliness. Her exercise-sculpted body was part and parcel of the fierceness, but her arms were what got the most attention in the press, to the point where paparazzi hung around outside her gym, hoping to capture a photo of her post-workout biceps.)

Madonna had originally considered naming the album *Black Madonna* and appearing on the sleeve in blackface, with red lips and white eyes, emulating a medieval representation of the Virgin Mary. The idea was abandoned after she decided the controversy it would generate wouldn't be worth it. But if she'd decided to go through with it, she could hardly have looked fiercer than she does on the *Hard Candy* cover. There's just one jarring note on the cover: a sticker advertising all the guest talent on the record. It announces that '4 Minutes' features Timberlake and Timbaland, that 'Beat Goes On' includes MCing from Kanye West and

Left Above: Madonna at Olympia Hall, Paris, telling the crowd she was honoured to be on the stage where Edith Piaf sang.

Right: Carrying off the rock guitar, biceps and Kabbalah bracelet look as only Madonna can at the Estadio Nacional de Chile in December 2008.

Overleaf: The Sticky & Sweet 85-date world tour was divided up into "Pimp", "Old School", "Gypsy" and "Rave" sections.

> ## "This song is for the emotionally retarded. Maybe you know some people who fall into that category. I know I do."
>
> *Madonna*

that the rest of the record includes "songs produced by the Neptunes, Timbaland and Justin Timberlake".

A necessary attention-grabbing device, it probably reeled in people who didn't realize Timberlake et al. were on the record, and who wouldn't have otherwise bought a Madonna record, but it was rather dispiriting. There was a core fanbase who could be relied on to buy the new album, but in order to bump up sales, her cool-cat collaborators had to be flagged up.

Having said that, the cool cats themselves were delighted to be on a Madonna album. In early 2007, a year before *Hard Candy* came out, Timbaland revealed that he'd tried to contact her with a view toward her working on his own album, *Shock Value*, only to learn that she in turn was hoping he'd agree to lend his skills to *Hard Candy*. In the end, she didn't appear on *Shock Value*, but Mosley made it onto five *Hard Candy* tracks, co-producing and -writing with Madonna and Justin Timberlake, among others.

As for Timberlake, the boy-bander-turned-R&B-star was a favourite of Madonna's. She loved his *FutureSex/LoveSounds* – the album that produced the incredibly moreish single 'SexyBack' and which is his biggest-selling LP to date. Timbaland, aka Virginia-born Tim Mosley, who was much fêted for his innovative minimalist approach to hip hop, had been the main co-producer on *FutureSex*, creating a distinctive

sound that was both funk and rock. It was the funk aspect that appealed to Madonna, and that was what Timba and Timber created on *Hard Candy*. (When the album was nearly finished, Timbaland paid it the ultimate accolade, declaring it "up there" with *FutureSex*.)

The cast list also included Pharrell Williams, then flying high as half of the production duo the Neptunes, and the exceedingly well-connected producer Nate "Danja" Hills. In essence, she'd assembled a writing/production dream team – and, unusually, an already famous one at that. Using Williams, West, Danja, Timber and Timba went against Madonna's normal policy of highlighting new talent, but one of her perpetual strengths has been choosing the right people for the right project, and for the urban sound she wanted to achieve with *Hard Candy*, she recognized that the best people were established beat-makers. "They're very opinionated. They're all stars in their own right," she told the *Sunday Telegraph*'s Jonathon Moran. "Pharrell and Justin are also vocalists" – which threw her at first. They gave her singing advice, and, she wryly said, no producer had ever told her how to sing before. Timberlake was so confident about what he could bring to the album that he saw *Hard Candy* almost as a companion album to *FutureSex*, revealing that he and Timbaland used the same production tricks as on *FutureSex*, and simply added Madonna to the mix.

As with *Confessions on a Dance Floor*, *Hard Candy* is mainly dedicated to fun, with a little wistfulness thrown in. The lustrous 'Miles Away' alludes to the difficulty of keeping a long-distance relationship going; the percolating 'Dance 2Night' is one of her now standard reflections on fame; and there seems to be a message to her soon-to-be-estranged husband in the gothic melancholy of 'Devil Wouldn't Recognize You'.

But there's also sex aplenty: opening track 'Candy Shop' seductively lists all the sweets on offer in her store (from chocolate to lollipops), but if that's too subtle, 'Incredible' bluntly states that having sex with her inamorata is pretty good.

But the most compelling song is the retro house stomper 'She's Not Me'. On one level, it's a hands-off warning to a love rival, but on another she's broadcasting a simple truth to the world: your Britneys and Rihannas and Katy Perrys are all very well, but there's

only one Madonna. She's part of pop's DNA, and don't forget it: she is M-Dolla.

But, heartfelt as the album was, it falls into the category headed "Less Than The Sum of its Parts" (which also includes her other overtly R&B LP, *Bedtime Stories*). There were few unequivocally positive reviews. "The album unfurls artfully...she manages to stamp the work with her own indelible mark," allowed Joan Anderman of the *Boston Globe*, and Dan Nishimoto of *Prefix* lauded her for creating a commercial version of the hip-hop/dance hybrid then dominating the American underground.

But the main gripe, repeated in many reviews, was that she'd let her producers lead the way, making her almost a guest on her own record. "Mediocre", "recycled pop", "well-intentioned failure" – disappointment was inscribed into these reviews, though more in sorrow than in anger.

Nonetheless, it sold 100,000 copies in American in its first day alone, pinged into the chart at Number 1 in 37 countries and became the eleventh bestselling album worldwide in 2008. As of 2012, its global sales total was 4 million copies. On the other hand, its singles fared less well. With the exception of '4 Minutes', a Top 3 smash in a dozen countries and a UK Number 1, *Hard Candy* produced no significant hits. The second single, 'Give it 2 Me', just made the UK Top 10 but stopped outside the American Top 50; and the third, 'Miles Away' – which had received favourable critical feedback – was the lowest-charting UK single of her career. After a run of 63 Top 20 singles in Britain, it crept to Number 39 – but even that eclipses its performance in America, where it didn't chart at all.

By the time 'Miles Away' was released, in October 2008, Madonna and Ritchie had announced their separation, and the pretty, Spanish-inflected tune seemed to acquire a different hue for her. Written as a despairing love note to someone who expressed love only when the pair were thousands of miles apart, it now represented a relationship that couldn't be fixed. It turned up on the setlist of the Sticky & Sweet Tour, and when she played Boston, she introduced it with, "This song is for the emotionally retarded. Maybe you know some people who fall into that category. I know I do."

But she would learn lessons, take time to absorb them and return in 2012, defiantly unbowed. She was, after all, M-Dolla.

Left: Madonna at the *Filth and Wisdom* screening, New York. Her next major film directing project was the royal biopic *W.E.*

CHAPTER 13
MDNA

Bruised by her divorce from Guy Ritchie and aware that younger artists were circling her throne, Madonna adopted a generic dance sound that divided critics. Even the presence of MIA and Nicki Minaj didn't help – at 2 million copies, it's her lowest seller.

2012 saw Madonna return for her
12th studio album. Less revolutionary
than her previous releases, it recorded
her lowest album sales to date.

MDNA

The @madonna era: she embraces social media and learns what not to say; and reunites with Billy Bubbles for her first album in four years (announced via Facebook, obviously).

By January 2012, Madonna had a Facebook page, and in March of that year she opened a Twitter account. She's taken to social media with the same diligence she's always applied to popular culture: if it's shaping the way the public thinks, she wants to know about it and then use it for her own ends. Under the name @madonna, she's proved an infrequent but enthusiastic tweeter, using the service to transmit her thoughts about politics and music, sometimes in the form of gnomic inspirational messages but often as straight-up joshing.

An example of the latter is this tweet, from April 2012: "#Obama2012, are you coming to my show in Washington DC? Make a girl from Detroit happy." There's no record of President Obama having attended either of the Washington shows of her MDNA Tour, which were in September of that year; he may have been otherwise occupied on the re-election trail. But she was unoffended, and on election night, she took several minutes out of her Pittsburgh concert to thank fans for voting for Obama. "Have you noticed that Obama rhymes with Madonna?" she asked mischievously. "It's going to be a great four years because we are going to have a great president in the White House." Not everyone in the crowd was a fan of the president, but she took their aggrieved shouts in her stride. "I love you, too," she said graciously.

Obama, by the way, was the first American president to be younger than her, albeit only by three years. This rather sobering fact may have led her to reflect that her career had now spanned five presidencies, which technically qualified her for an Elder Stateswoman of Pop medal. But of the artists born, like her, in 1958 – among them Kate Bush, Prince, Anita Baker and Paul Weller – she's also the only one not to have lost touch with the pop instinct.

Her need, first and foremost, is to siphon her experiences into three-minute songs, and being fluent in this genre means that since 1982, every successive generation of teenagers has grown up with Madonna in the charts. For the teenager of the 2010s, who discovers music on YouTube and Spotify, "the charts" don't have the same significance. But even if there is a change to the way a song's popularity is calculated, it's a fairly safe bet that she'll be prominent in whatever system replaces the current Top 40.

She's also become an avid Instagrammer, posting photos of her travels, her outfits and her children – Rocco and Lourdes are now startlingly grown-up. Social media is a natural outlet for her, conveying her opinions directly to fans and allowing instantaneous feedback. She's got herself in hot water a few times, however, by misjudging

Above Right: Madonna stands tall at the MDNA North America tour opener on August 28, 2012 in Philadelphia.

Right: The 2012 MDNA Tour was the second-highest-grossing tour by a female artist – behind her own Sticky & Sweet Tour.

"*I need to move.
I need to sweat.
I need to make
new music!*"

Madonna

the public's tolerance on certain issues. In early 2014, she posted a photo of 13-year-old Rocco holding a bottle of gin, with the caption "The party has just begun! Bring it! 2014". This provoked accusations that she was encouraging underage drinking – to which she replied, quite reasonably, that they'd been messing around and nobody had been drinking. "Calm down and get a sense of humor!" she urged, probably unsuccessfully.

A few weeks later, she made a more serious error of judgment, hashtagging a photo of Rocco in a boxing ring with a racial slur. Condemnation was immediate, and she swiftly removed the photo and issued a statement. "I am sorry if I offended anyone with my use of the N-word on Instagram. I am not a racist. There's no way to defend the use of the word. It was all about intention. It was used as a term of endearment toward my son who is white. I appreciate that it's a provocative word and I apologize if it gave people the wrong impression. Forgive me." This fanned the flames of opprobrium even higher, and she added another comment, which sounded far more like the Madonna of old: "Ok let me start this again. #get off of my dick haters."

Both photos certainly lay her open to the charge of being an embarrassing mum, as does her failure to foresee the effect of her words, but it was obvious that her intention hadn't been to offend. The wording of her apology shows she knew that she'd made a mistake, and will know better next time. What was unexpected was her humbled request "Forgive me"; she'd rarely said that before. Her humility and sensitivity to public opinion were signs of another, more internal, reinvention.

Just two years before, she'd issued another near-unprecedented apology. It was in February 2012, just before the release of *MDNA*, her twelfth and most recent album. She'd been booked into the halftime slot at the Super Bowl, held that year in Indianapolis – one of the most coveted promotional platforms for any artist because TV viewing figures are traditionally in the area of 100 million.

The show was a convenient way of promoting not just the album but her new single, 'Give Me All Your Luvin'' and an 88-date tour scheduled for that summer. 'Give Me All Your Luvin'' featured American rapper Nicki Minaj and British rapper/singer MIA, and both women appeared

"I am sorry if I offended anyone... I apologize if it gave people the wrong impression. Forgive me."
Madonna

with her at the Super Bowl, dressed as cheerleaders. All proceeded to plan until, halfway through the song, MIA flipped her middle finger at the camera. It was more incongruous than offensive; until that instant, she had been amiably shaking her cheerleader pom-poms. It was so quick that many missed it, but broadcaster NBC issued a pre-emptive apology: "Our system was late to obscure the inappropriate gesture and we apologize to our viewers".

A Madonna show without controversy is like a day without sunshine, and as "controversy" went, MIA's finger was mild stuff. The remarkable thing, though, was that Madonna was unhappy about it. In what must have been a first, she admitted to radio host Ryan Seacrest that she'd found it "out of place". Though the gesture was "kind of punk rock", she was annoyed that it had detracted from a performance otherwise marked by "love and good energy." It was, she complained, "such a teenager...thing to do." Some critics were taken aback by her apparent volte-face; the Madonna of the 80s and 90s would never have taken umbrage at another artist expressing herself, however crudely. But her goalposts had evidently shifted;

Left: The theme of the 88-date MDNA Tour was the journey from darkness to light.

the right to self-expression now had to be balanced against whether the shock it would cause was worth it.

Whatever the case, her 12-minute performance was watched by a TV audience of 114 million (a record for a Super Bowl halftime show at the time, though it was broken by Bruno Mars two years later). It had the desired effect on sales, too. 'Give Me All Your Luvin'', a bubbly rave-pop number praised as "impossibly fun" by the *NME*'s Priya Elan, reached Number 10 in the US (though it didn't do much in the UK, where it halted at Number 37), and *MDNA*, which followed in March, debuted at the top of the *Billboard* chart.

MDNA's opening-week sales of 359,000 were her best since *Music*'s first week in 2000. Some suggested, however, that she had benefited from "ticket-bundling", which gave a copy of the album to people buying tickets for the MDNA Tour. It's true that around 185,000 of *MDNA*'s sales were achieved that way – but the tickets were priced to include the cost of the album, so the LP wasn't a free giveaway, and Madonna had earned that 359,000 figure. (The figure did, however, drop substantially in the second week, falling to Number 8 in the US chart, with just 48,000 sales.)

The title *MDNA* – it had been changed from the provisional *LUV* – generated much debate among fans. Some presumed it was simply a hipster-style abbreviation of her name – rather like MIA, whose real name is Maya – while others contended that it stood for "Madonna's DNA". Many pointed out its similarity to MDMA, the chemical name for ecstasy. The matter was resolved when the album's co-producer, Martin Solveig, told the *New York Post*'s Mandy Stadtmiller that MIA herself had suggested the title as "a really good abbreviation" of Madonna's name. There was no intention, he said, of promoting drugs, "except for the harmless and pure, exciting drugs, like music."

Yet the cover art might be taken as promoting some sort of hallucinatory experience – it shows her face divided into prism-like vertical strips – and the track listing does include a song called 'I'm Addicted', a festival-style rave-up that ends with the chant "MDNA! MDNA!". While we're at it, the credits, which run to three solid pages of tiny type, are arranged in a solid black of text with no paragraphs or spaces, so that deciphering them brings on a kind of pie-eyed stupor in itself.

But it's rather more likely that the cover photo was simply Madonna being mischievous rather than inviting buyers to get high. She's never advocated substance misuse, and her own lifestyle, with its emphasis on yoga and healthy eating, has verged on straight edge at times. Even so, an anti-drug group called Cannabis Skunk Sense obligingly reacted, calling the title "ill-advised", as if children would automatically interpret it as a cue to buy ecstasy in the playground. If anything, it would have had the opposite effect, as most self-respecting adolescents run a mile from anything adults consider cool.

Far Left: Though the *MDNA* album was relatively unsuccessful, Madonna's reputation for spectacular shows meant the tour sold out instantly.

Left: Madonna's Super Bowl halftime show on February 5, 2012 attracted a record 114 million TV viewers.

Below: Madonna's high-school cheerleading experience came in handy for this majorette-themed version of 'Express Yourself' performed in Rome.

Overleaf: For the first time, Madonna (here in Buenos Aires, December 2012) used social media to publicize the tour.

> ## *"I'm on the lookout for the maddest, sickest, most bad ass people to collaborate with."*
>
> ### *Madonna*

A final note on the cover: fans loved it. A trawl through UKMix.org – an online meeting place for hundreds of her European admirers – unearths the same comments, over and over: "Great", "Love the colours", "Hot". A few naysayers compared it to a Kylie Minogue sleeve – though why would that be a bad thing? But one point on which most were agreed was that they preferred it to *Hard Candy*'s cover photo. The ultra-toned physique she'd displayed there had left many cold, and had been unfavourably compared to her softer look on the *Ray of Light* sleeve. The consensus was that golden hair and soft-focus prettiness suited her better than platinum blonde and hard edges.

The other song titles made it clear that this wasn't a "drug" album. 'Girl Gone Wild', 'Gang Bang', 'I Don't Give A', 'Turn Up the Radio', 'I'm a Sinner', 'I Fucked Up'... pretty well made it clear that Madonna's focus was, as ever, sexual politics, personal issues – and dancing. She'd implied as much back in December 2010, when she'd announced via Facebook that she was in the early stages of making a new album. "It's official!" she wrote. "I need to move. I need to sweat. I need to make new music! Music I can dance to. I'm on the lookout for the maddest, sickest, most bad ass people to collaborate with. I'm just saying ..." The announcement generated more than 5,000 comments from around the world, including one from a woman who simply typed dozens of pink hearts.

The reason for needing to move and sweat was that she'd spent the previous two years making a movie. Directed, produced and co-written by her, *W.E.* was a big-budget bio-drama about Edward VIII's romance with Wallis Simpson. The story must have struck a chord with her – American woman shakes the world of a quintessentially English chap – and she poured herself into the project. "I had the same kind of pressure when I began my music career," she said when the film was shown at the Toronto International Film Festival in September 2011. "I didn't know what to expect. I had to earn my way [to] being taken seriously in the music department, and now I'm well aware that I have to do the same in the world of film."

The odd good notice aside ("...if people were to watch it with no knowledge of who directed, they would be pleasantly surprised," was the opinion of the *Daily Mail*'s Baz Bamigboye), reviews were unfavourable, and box-office takings were equally disappointing.

Where *W.E.* did make its mark was at the 2012 Golden Globes, where one of the songs from its soundtrack, 'Masterpiece', won the Best Original Song award. An airy ballad accented by Spanish guitar, it was well-liked by reviewers, and even judged by the *Guardian*'s Michael Cragg to be "one of the best vocal performances on the album." The album referred to was *MDNA*, to which it had been added, presumably because having an award-winning song on the record would do its chances no harm at all.

Co-written with William Orbit – their first collaboration since the *Music* era – 'Masterpiece' was her first piece of new music in nearly four years. But, having been created for *W.E.*, it's a touch out of place on *MDNA* – at least, it's fair to say that it sounds like nothing else on the album. With the exception of closing track 'Falling Free' – a stately folk ballad that conjures up Kate Bush and Enya – the majority of *MDNA* is bass-heavy arena-pop. From its opening number, 'Girl Gone Wild' (whose title was lifted from an adult-film franchise), it's immensely energetic, a clubbing-all-night set that follows the peak-after-peak sequencing of *Confessions on a Dance Floor*.

She had a reason to put her most youthful face forward. In the four years since *Hard Candy*, a genuine competitor had emerged. Lady Gaga was, in early 2012, the biggest name in American pop, with 21 million album sales to her credit – and she was distinctly different from other young female artists. Like the rookie Madonna in 1982, Gaga had a plan – an aesthetic. The author interviewed Gaga for the *Guardian* in 2008 and was struck by the similarity to Madonna in her early days. From that interview:

There is something of the young Madonna about Gaga: she's boundlessly ambitious and emphatically denies she is a record-company construct. "To be quite honest," she says, "the label had to tone me down. You'd think they were giving me tiny shorts to put on, but it was the other way around. When they met me, I was working in a nightclub in New York, half naked, but I had a big voice and they liked me. If anything, they put more clothes on me." An encounter with Gaga is a bracing experience, and you come away heartened at the prospect of people like her in the charts.

With her awareness of the pop climate, Madonna would have known that Gaga's quirk-driven version of EDM was shaping the way the charts sounded. She would also have realized that Gaga was seen by many as her successor. The words "the new Madonna" popped up in a good few Gaga reviews, the first time any new artist had been seen as a serious contender. There was, for the first time in years, something to prove. As Andy Gill said in the *Independent*, "*MDNA* represents a determined, no-nonsense restatement of the Madonna brand following the lacklustre *Hard Candy*."

To make the album, she selected a team of European producers. The idea was to move on from the sound created by the All-American big-hitters she'd used on *Hard Candy*. Thus, Billy Bubbles (aka Orbit) was back with a bang. Since making his name on *Ray of Light*, he'd released three solo albums and worked with a panoply of big names, from Blur to Beck, but Madonna still considered him a musical soul mate, describing their collaborations as "magic". And their reunion was fruitful: his name appears on six *MDNA* tracks, of which a highlight is 'I'm a Sinner', fuelled by an Indian motif that recalls *Ray of Light*.

But the album's three major tracks – the ones that appeared as singles – were overseen by Italian DJ Benny Benassi ('Girl Gone Wild') and French producer Martin Solveig ('Give Me All Your Luvin'' and 'Turn Up the Radio'). The pair were big names in dance music (and Solveig had had pop success with the twee 2010 single 'Hello') but were unknown to the mainstream. This was the first superstar project for both.

And they put their backs into it. As Madonna told reporters at the Golden Globes after she'd picked up her trophy for 'Masterpiece', "I did a good majority of the record with Martin Solveig. I love his sound. It's really fresh – it doesn't sound like anybody else. He's brilliantly talented.

Right: Madonna's skimpy costume caused an uproar in Istanbul, where she revealed one of her breasts.

Below: The MDNA World Tour consisted of 88 dates, including an outdoor event in London's Hyde Park in July 2012.

I would say his music is happy – it puts a smile on your face and my record does that too." Orbit, however, brought out her reflective side: "And I collaborated again with William Orbit, who tends to make me more introspective. His songs tend to be...I don't want to say dark, but more thoughtful and introspective. So, yeah, it's a good combination of the light and the dark."

Recruiting America's most successful female rapper, Nicki Minaj, for two tracks ('Give Me All Your Luvin'' and 'I Don't Give A') was criticized by some as blatantly courting the teenage dollar, but Minaj's presence made sense. Her adrenalized, Day-Glo flow was like an electrical charge, vividly complementing Madonna's sugar-sweet singing. Minaj later revealed in an interview with *Complex* magazine that she'd prepared by watching the *Truth or Dare* documentary but had still been bowled over by the extent of Madonna's involvement in the studio. She was the only "humongous" star who'd stayed in the studio with Minaj during the entire recording process. Minaj's two-word summing up of the whole experience: "Freaking amazing."

The sparkle of Minaj's two songs makes a case for Madonna working with more female artists – something she's rarely done. In fact, *MDNA* breaks new ground for her there, featuring no fewer than three collaborations with women: along with Minaj and MIA – the latter a

Left: The MDNA Tour was divided into themes of 'Transgression', 'Prophecy', 'Masculine/Feminine' and 'Redemption'.

Above: 2012 saw Madonna launch Moscow's Hard Candy fitness club. The chain now has eight locations.

subdued contrast to Minaj – there's also a sleeve credit for one "Lola Leon". Her daughter contributes backing vocals to the bubbly pop-rock ditty 'Superstar', and proves a chip off the old block, her voice blending so seamlessly with her mother's that it's hard to tell who's who.

On her two preceding albums, Madonna had got into the habit of slipping highly personal lyrics, often pertaining to her marriage, underneath the beats. As her first post-divorce record, *MDNA* revealed some livid mental bruises: the crunchy electro-thud of 'I Don't Give A' conceals a rancorous polemic about how hard it is to move on after a break-up. She seems angrier at herself than at her ex-husband; it may be the only song in pop that contains the word "pre-nup". Similarly, 'Love Spent' had a sting in its delicate orchestral tail, revealing that being the partner with the higher income had made things difficult. And 'Gang Bang' is a kill-you-dead number that isn't necessarily about the marriage, but does use gunshot noises that wouldn't have been out of place in one of Ritchie's gangland flicks.

Overall, Madonna gave *MDNA* her all. She hadn't forgotten that the core of her empire – which as of 2014 encompasses fashion and perfume ranges, a chain of Hard Candy gyms and a skin-care line – was music, and when it came to music, there were no half-measures.

The reviews, when they arrived, acknowledged that. Whether positive or negative, they allowed that there was still no one like her. There was the odd rapturous notice ("Her best since, in all sincerity, the career high of 1998's *Ray of Light*," asserted *Q* magazine's Simon Goddard), a few so-so ones ("...[not] the return to form she thinks it is." said the *Guardian's* Alexis Petridis) and a much larger sheaf that praised it, with reservations. But the theme running through all was that she was still the greatest female pop icon and that whether a Madonna record was brilliant or disappointing, it still mattered.

MDNA is her lowest-selling album. Despite debuting at Number 1 in both the US and the UK, it had sold less than 2 million copies worldwide by the end of 2012. One theory has it that she didn't do enough promotion in the weeks before the album was released, but the real reason is probably more prosaic – that it didn't connect with enough people. The Top 10 success of 'Give Me All Your Luvin'' didn't stop the two subsequent singles from being relative chart failures – although, as ever, they hit Number 1 in the *Billboard* dance chart. Whatever else happens, she continues to make people dance.

By contrast, the 2012 MDNA Tour was a huge success, grossing $305 million, making it the tenth biggest tour of all time. And, as of spring 2014, the internet is abuzz with rumours of her next album. (She's teasingly revealed that she's been working with Swedish DJ Avicii and American producer Diplo.) The public will always want to know, and hear. She is, after all, Madonna.

Far Left: Madonna strikes a balletic pose in Philadelphia, the week after her 54th birthday.

Left: Dressed to impress and to get the press's attention, Madonna attends at the New York premiere of the concert film *Madonna: The MDNA Tour* in June 2013.

CHAPTER 14

REBEL HEART

After the sales disappointment of Hard Candy and MDNA, Madonna returns with what looks to be a lucky 13 – her thirteenth studio album. Critics praise her honesty about the breakup of her relationship with Brahim Zaibat – but a spill at the Brit Awards grabs the headlines.

Madonna absorbs the spotlight while performing *Rebel Heart*'s 'Living For Love' during the Grammys, Los Angeles, February 8, 2015.

REBEL HEART

Leaks, tumbles and social-media mistakes crop up, but 2015's Rebel Heart *is her best album since* Confessions on a Dance Floor.

"It was a horrible nightmare, because I like to be amazing," Madonna told chat-show host Jonathan Ross in February 2015. The "nightmare" had happened 24 hours before, at the Brit Awards in London, as she performed her new single, 'Living for Love'. The first official taste of her thirteenth studio album, *Rebel Heart*, the song demanded a suitably spectacular premiere, and she concocted one. What went wrong was the cape she wore.

She was a special guest at the Brits – not nominated for an award, but given a slot to perform her first single in nearly three years. The stage was a-swarm with dancers dressed as bullfighters and bulls; stalking up a walkway, in toreador pants and hooded black cape, was Madonna herself. She made an imperious entrance, her cape's 4.5-metre (15-foot) train carried by two bullfighters. As she reached a short flight of stairs, she tried to unfasten the cape to allow it to be pulled away by a bull. (When Madonna puts on a production, she puts on a production.) It was tied so tightly at the neck that she couldn't get it loose, and when the bull reached for it, she was pulled backwards, along with the cape.

The footage of her fall, which became an instant online sensation, shows her tumbling down the steps, where she's surrounded by concerned dancers. Swiftly pulling herself together, she rises and sings the rest of the song, which – and this sparked accusations that it was all a stunt – happened to be about falling down and getting up again.

Was it a stunt, Ross asked her when she appeared on his show the next night. She shook her head vehemently: of course it wasn't a stunt. After her fall, she'd had to be monitored overnight for signs of concussion. "I smacked the back of my head, so there was a man standing over me with a flashlight till about 3 a.m., making sure I was still compos mentis," she said. "I'm always nervous [before appearing on television]. Live TV is an ucker." (Yes, she said "ucker". There was a time when she would have put an "f" in front of it, but she's less confrontational about the small stuff now, saving her energy for bigger battles.)

Moreover, if it was a stunt, it backfired. For a week afterwards, Madonna was a trending topic on social media, but nobody was discussing her music. Nearly all the commentary focused on the fall, and what it portended. There was plenty of age-related mockery along the lines of this comment, posted on YouTube: "A woman her age should be more careful on steps. I am forever warning my mother." Trollish views like those were countered by pro-Madonna comments noting that this was ageism in its full glory, being used to belittle a powerful woman. Others, meanwhile, were impressed by her fitness: she was 56, had sustained a whack to the head and still managed to keep singing. Talk about aplomb.

Right: Madonna attended the Grammys dressed as a matador. She was the first performer of the evening at the 2015 event.

Far Right: The singer appears on a Madonna-only special edition of *The Jonathan Ross Show*, London, March 14, 2015.

"It was a horrible
nightmare,
because I like
to be amazing."

Madonna

Far Left: Madonna, as ever, provides the spectacular. Part of her 2015 Grammys performance saw her suspended high above the Staples Center stage.

Left: The fall that echoed around the world. Madonna and *that* slip at the BRIT Awards, February 25, 2015. It got everyone talking but not about *Rebel Heart*.

Below: "I need a partner in my life." Madonna confessed she yearns for love after her split with Brahim Zaibat, after three years.

"Really? Is that how it's broken down? I'm so stupid. I didn't know it was anything to do with my age. I just do my work." Madonna

Aplomb was the word. Rather than behaving as most mortals would, which would have been to lie down and cry, she ended the song by triumphantly raising a pair of bull's horns above her head. Speaking to Ross the next night, she attributed her instant recovery to "core strength" – so all that yoga had served a purpose – and knowing how to fall. She'd fallen many times from her horse, she said.

To reinforce the message that the whole thing was just an irritating mishap, she posted a note to her 3.6 million Instagram followers: "Armani hooked me up! My beautiful cape was tied too tight! But nothing can stop me and love really lifted me up! Thanks for your good wishes! I'm fine! #livingforlove".

(The publicity didn't help the prospects of 'Living for Love', by the way; it didn't chart at all in the US and reached only Number 26 in the UK. That chart position wasn't helped by Radio 1 declining to play it. The explanation offered by the station's Head of Music, George Ergatoudis, was that Radio 1 needed to attract younger listeners, whereas "the vast majority of people who like Madonna, who like her music now, are over 30 and frankly, we've moved on from Madonna." A bemused Madonna later said: ""Really? Is that how it's broken down? I'm so stupid. I didn't know it was anything to do with my age. I just do my work.")

The Brits incident was the climax of a difficult couple of months. In November 2014, two songs from the new album – the title track and 'Wash All Over Me' – were leaked online, followed by 11 unfinished demos several weeks later and 14 more on Christmas Day. Furious, she Instagrammed: "I have been violated as a human and an artist! #fuckedupshit", and later labelled the leak "a form of terrorism" and "artistic rape". Though she quickly deleted that post, the clamour caused by her intemperate use of "rape" and "terrorism" inspired an article in the *Guardian* with the wry title "Please, Madonna, step away from your smartphone".

On December 20, feeling backed into a corner, she brought forward *Rebel Heart*'s release date to March 6, and released six tracks online herself: 'Living for Love', 'Devil Pray', 'Ghosttown', 'Unapologetic Bitch', 'Illuminati' and 'Bitch I'm Madonna'. With the free tracks – which were given away with every pre-order of *Rebel Heart* – came this statement: "I was hoping to release my new single 'Living for Love' on Valentine's Day with the rest of the album coming in the Spring, I would prefer my fans to hear completed versions of some of the songs instead of the incomplete tracks that are circulating. Please consider these six songs as an early Christmas gift." You can practically sense the gritted teeth, but making them available herself did at least gave her some control over the situation.

(In January 2015 the Israeli police announced that its cybercrime branch had arrested a man, alleging that he'd hacked Madonna's computer as well as "the personal computers of several international artists over the past few months" and stolen unreleased tracks from all, which were then sold.)

Madonna had been a longtime critic of illegal file-sharing; in 2003, when the title track of *American Life* was leaked by MP3 sites, she made her feelings clear by sending a track to the sites herself. Disguised as another version of the song 'American Life', it featured a recorded message of the singer herself, acerbically asking: "What the fuck do you think you're doing?" By 2014, the music industry's view of file-sharing had changed, with many artists habitually releasing free songs in order to promote a forthcoming album. Now Madonna was reluctantly joining their ranks.

She was at least rewarded by landing Number 1 slots on the daily iTunes chart in 41 countries. Nonetheless, she was deeply unhappy that she'd been forced to share the music before it was ready. This wasn't what she'd planned, she told *Billboard*. She'd always worked to a strict timetable when she released a record, first putting out the single, then making a video, and, finally, starting the long haul of publicizing the album.

She'd been working on *Rebel Heart* since early 2014, with a cast of producers and songwriters that included Kanye West, Nicki Minaj, Diplo and Avicii. (Another co-writer, on the track 'Holy Water', was

British singer Natalia Kills, who later became a judge on the New Zealand version of *The X Factor* and earned brief notoriety when she and her songwriter husband, Willy Moon, criticized a contestant so scathingly that they were fired from the show.)

There were guest spots, too, from Alicia Keys, Chance the Rapper, Nas and, surprisingly, Mike Tyson. The controversial ex-boxer, who'd known the singer since meeting her and Sean Penn in 1988, contributed a spoken-word prelude to the song 'Iconic'. "I just go in there and start talking," he told *Rolling Stone*. "I'm talking about my life and things that I have endured ... It was really intense." His 12-second segment, in which he affirms his greatness, initially seems like grandiose bluster, but does make sense in the context of the track. It's one of Madonna's more fiery motivational numbers – an anthemic club track that wags its finger in the listener's face, exhorting him/her to discover their inner hero.

Pointing out that the words "I can't" are only a letter or so removed from "icon", the song is preachy but impassioned. Madonna's voice, laden with electronic effects, is insistent, demanding that listeners not be daunted by failure. She alludes to Muhammad Ali's immortal "float like a butterfly" comment, building into a quivering electro-crescendo. To all this, Chance the Rapper adds a reflective verse about bending superstardom to one's will – using it to change the world rather than to be crushed by it.

All told, 'Iconic' is reminiscent of the *Like a Virgin* song 'Over and Over', with added wisdom. While 'Over and Over' was her speaking to herself, pushing herself to be spectacular, 'Iconic' takes that internal positivity and aims it outward: you, too, can be spectacular. But there's spectacular – and there's Madonna. It's fine for everyday Joes to trundle along, floating like butterflies, but none of us will ever nail it quite the way she does.

Two tracks on *Rebel Heart* make that clear: 'Unapologetic Bitch' is one, the other is 'Bitch I'm Madonna'. Just take in the latter title. Bitch, she's Madonna. There's no answer to that. It's as if she's summed up her influence on culture in three words – look on her works, ye Mighty, and despair. The song itself, however, isn't a queenly glide but a manic EDM track about partying all night, complete with a ripping verse from Nicki Minaj. The picture it paints, of a house party where

guests end up in the pool fully clothed, drinking booze out of each other's shoes, is actually reminiscent of Katy Perry's 2011 hit 'Last Friday Night'. But Perry herself was influenced by Madonna, so you could say it's a case of things coming full circle.

'Unapologetic Bitch', meanwhile, is her riposte to anyone who expects her to be ashamed of her actions. Specifically, it's a long-delayed response to *Playboy* and *Penthouse* magazines, which published nude photos of her in July 1985, when she was reaching peak fame. The black-and-white pictures (which had been taken in 1978, during a stint as an artist's model) were, as the news site Salon.com recently put it, "pretty normcore" – though she was completely naked in most, they were almost prim. Well, prim compared to what would appear several years later in *Sex*. At the time, however, the magazines played them for all they were worth – *Playboy*'s coverline read: "Unlike a virgin ... for the very first time".

As she told *Billboard*'s Keith Caulfield, she had refused to give *Playboy* and *Penthouse* the reaction they wanted, which was to see her "cower [ing] in shame". Cower in shame? Not in 1985 and not now. Her response 30 years ago was that she had nothing to be ashamed of, and 'Unapologetic Bitch' is a kind of belated postscript to that – her own 'Je Ne Regrette Rien'.

Anyway, while the nude-photos incident is the inspiration behind the song, you wouldn't necessarily know that from the lyric, which is clearly directed at a recent ex-boyfriend. Gossips claimed it was her former dancer, Brahim Zaibat, whom she dated from 2010 to 2013. She has rarely talked about him, but in 2012, during an interview on the American news programme *Nightline*, she said: "I didn't write down on a piece of paper, 'I'm now going to have a relationship with a younger man.' That's just what happened. You see, that's the romantic in me – I just met someone that I cared for, and this happened to be his age [he was then 24]. I don't want to live my life on my own. I love being a mother. My children fill me up in many ways, and inspire me in many ways, but I need a partner in my life and I think most people feel that way."

'Unapologetic Bitch' has a fairly standard Madonna post-relationship lyric: at the outset, she's wounded, even distraught, but quickly bounces back; she blocks the ex when he tries to phone her, scathingly notes

that he was never all that in the bedroom and reminds him that she's very rich and he's not. The Diplo-produced track is a joyous noisefest, weaving rave-style airhorn into a ska rhythm.

"I was Googling her while I was working with her, and she's literally sold, like, 300 million copies of songs," Diplo told Kathy Iandolf of the music site Idolator, in an interview halfway through the *Rebel Heart* recording sessions. That rather prompts the question: how did Diplo – one of the most respected songwriter/producers currently working – not already know that? But that assumes too much; Diplo was born in 1978 and grew up at a time when Madonna was never off the radio or MTV, and her ubiquity perhaps made him take her for granted.

By the same token, the monstrously successful Swedish DJ/producer Avicii, who was born in the year *Like a Prayer* was released, may not have realized exactly how ground-breaking and culturally significant she's been. Indeed, it's likely that most people who grew up in the '90s or '00s are unaware of how different expectations of women were before she became famous. As a *Guardian* reader called ArundelXVI remarked on the paper's website soon after *Rebel Heart's* release: "I don't think Young People Today really get how huge she was, and how fun her music was."

Madonna herself seems to be casting the odd glance backwards these days. This message was posted on her Twitter, Instagram and Facebook accounts on April 11, 2015: "30 years ago today the Virgin Tour set Sail..............in the blink of an eye! So grateful!!!!!! Still a #rebelheart".

Avicii produced four songs on the 19-track "deluxe" edition of *Rebel Heart*: 'Devil Pray', 'Heartbreak City', 'Messiah' and the title track. (The 14-song standard edition contains only the first two.) 'Devil Pray' is especially fine – a countryish, gothicky sliver of a thing that has echoes of the 2000 single 'Don't Tell Me'. *Daily Telegraph* reviewer Neil McCormick wasn't a fan – "If we can overlook ludicrous techno folk song 'Devil Pray', in which Madonna informs us that drugs are bad, she has (mostly) checked her tendency to hectoring self-justification and holier-than-thou lecturing" – but other critics were impressed, with Amy Pettifier writing for The Quietus: "This is the first of many deft, warping, mood changes from acoustic to electro that populate the album...A precious little ghost in the machine."

But the most eyebrow-raising Avicii song didn't make it on to the album. Titled 'Two Steps Behind Me' (available on YouTube, as of this writing), it contemptuously addresses another woman who has copied her style. This rival dresses like Madonna, speaks like Madonna, walks like Madonna; throughout the song, she's dismissed as a "Wannabe", a reminder that people have been emulating Madonna since the original Wannabe era three decades ago. Responding to speculation, her manager, Guy Oseary, released an unequivocal denial via Twitter: "That song is NOT about Gaga or anyone in particular. The song is an unfinished demo she had no intention of finishing or releasing along with many others. She has NO ill will towards Gaga. It's nonsense. She

was listening to the Tony Bennett duet album [*Cheek to Cheek*, recorded by Bennett and Gaga in 2014] last week and appreciating it."

Gaga most certainly does get a mention on the *Rebel Heart* song 'Illuminati', however, along with Jay Z, Beyoncé, Oprah Winfrey and a dozen other household names. Madonna described the song as an attempt to reclaim the original meaning of "illuminati", which has been appropriated by conspiracy theorists to denote supposed secret groups of powerful individuals (reputed to include Jay Z, Beyoncé and, yes, Madonna). Her version sternly points out that the Illuminati were a culturally sophisticated, eighteenth-century bunch who used their power for good, and the song is a raucous knees-up of optimistic electronic squawks. In its review, Spin.com didn't especially like the tune, claiming it "flails in overwrought production, its lyrical power lost to thunks and howls that are a little too purposeful in their creepiness", but Annie Zaleski of A.V. Club found it "pleasingly confrontational" in parts.

As for the album in its entirety, the majority of reviews were positive. Despite disquiet over online images that showed the album's cover photo – Madonna's face bound with ties – transposed on to images of Martin Luther King and Nelson Mandela, some critics claimed *Rebel Heart* was the best thing she'd done in quite a few albums.

Jim Farber of New York's *Daily News* praised its unprecedented openness: Madonna admits to loneliness and experiencing the sting of rejection; the stately piano ballad 'Wash All Over Me' even appears to contemplate the end of her career. "It's hard to imagine Madonna expressing things like this before, let alone making them ring true," Faber wrote. "That's *Rebel Heart*'s peak feature: It presents a 58-year-old woman who, in the best possible sense, sounds her age." The *Boston Globe*'s James Reed was equally enthusiastic: "... call it a return to form since the album is her most satisfying effort in a decade and nimbly connects the dots between Madonna's various eras and guises."

The consensus is that the album, which peaked at Number 2 in Britain and the US, but reached Number 1 in a dozen countries shows her wielding her still-considerable power with maturity and grace "...the singer genuinely seems to be revealing her personal feelings and frailties," said the *Guardian*'s Alexis Petridis. "She can come up with songs that are both mature and reflective and that function as fantastic pop music, and they're all the more potent because they sound like they're being made entirely on her own terms."

Thirty-three years after the single 'Everybody' launched a career that eventually changed pop, feminism and the lives of millions of women, she's still doing it on her own terms.

Above Left: In the face of declining record sales, Madonna proved she is still a vibrant, and controversial, live performer.

Above Right: Thirteen studio albums and counting, Madonna remains a captivating spectacle for the press and public alike.

"It's time for me to take a different approach." Madonna

"Amid the Beyoncés, Taylors, Mileys and Gagas, where is Madonna's place in pop music?" mused the *Washington Post*'s Chris Kelly on September 13, 2015. The night before, Madonna had played Washington, DC's Verizon Center, the third show of the 82-date Rebel Heart Tour. Kelly wasn't much taken with *Rebel Heart* as an album – "anything but revolutionary" – but conceded that her on-stage offering was fantastic: she was still provocative, inventive and musically engaged. Her perch in pop's top tier remains secure by dint of the fact that, even after all these years, there's still nobody quite like her. Even Lady Gaga, who is often compared with Madonna, is no Madonna.

Nevertheless, these days the woman herself seems to be wondering about her place in pop. Her unprecedented success guarantees her a place in the history of Western culture – among her recent achievements, the Rebel Heart Tour grossed $170 million, retaining her status as the top-selling female live act in history - but she's in uncharted territory these days. She finds herself the rather ambivalent torchbearer for older women in pop, and at 60, she's looking to reinvent herself yet again to fit her new circumstances. Despite having diversified into film-making and political activism, her bread and butter is still music, and the challenge is to make songs with integrity, retaining the fizz of her best productions while recalibrating her image.

"To age [as a female musician] is a sin," she said in late 2016 as she accepted Billboard's Woman of the Year award. "You will be criticized, you will be vilified, and you will definitely not be played on the radio." Sixteen months later, she was still fighting the same battle. Early in 2018 she told *TheCut.com*: "What I am going through now is ageism, with people putting me down or giving me a hard time because I date younger men or do things that are considered to be only the domain of younger women." At about the same time, however, she suggested that it might be time to downsize her live shows. She had a hankering for intimacy, she said; after decades of splashy arena productions (the Rebel Heart Tour, for instance, featured 20 dancers, a recreation of the Last Supper and a segment where she played ukulele), she longed for something on a human scale.

"It's time for me to take a different approach and really get back down to the beauty and simplicity of music and lyrics," she told *Entertainment Weekly*. In March, 2016, at a gig in Melbourne, she offered an early sample of what that might entail. Instead of the usual whizz-bang arena set, she performed a special show titled Tears of a Clown, which she described as "performance art, comedy, story-telling and music, of course". The clown theme extended to her wardrobe: she arrived in a clown suit, pedalling a tricycle. That show was also notable for its reference to Rocco Ritchie, her son with Guy Ritchie. She and Guy were then waging a custody battle sparked by Rocco's refusal to live with his mother in New York. The 15-year-old wanted to stay with his father in London, and his parents launched litigation that ended with Rocco being allowed to remain with his father. At the Melbourne show, a photo of Rocco was beamed behind Madonna during the *American Life* song 'Intervention'.

Her nurturing side continued to express itself in 2017 and 2018. Early 2017 saw her adopt two more Malawian children – four-year-old twin sisters called Stella and Estere. Also that year, she and some of her family took up residence in Sintra, near Lisbon, where younger son David was training at the Benfica youth football academy. "I'm an official soccer mom," she quipped during a December appearance on the American chat show *Live with Kelly and Ryan*. "2017 was soccer mom in Portugal. 2018, I'm coming back, baby, and I'm coming for you!"

The very words fans wanted to hear. By the spring of 2018, two film-directing projects were taking shape. *Loved*, adapted from the novel *The Impossible Lives of Greta Wells*, had actually been in the works since 2013, when she bought the film rights ("It touches on a lot of really important topics: fighting for women's rights, gay rights, civil rights, always fighting for the underdog," she told *Harper's Bazaar*). The second project, *Taking Flight*, was also right up her street – it was the true story of Michaela DePrince, a Sierra Leone war orphan who became a renowned ballerina. More tantalisingly, she also hinted that she was working on an album. The online Madonnasphere was electrified by an Instagram post in April that seemed to confirm rumours that the follow-up to *Rebel Heart* was on the way. "No This is NOT my new music," she wrote. "But im having fun in the studio in between takes!! #music #mirwais #magic". Accompanying the post was a snippet of her singing an airy disco track. The suggestion that she was again working with Mirwais, co-producer of her best 21st-century albums – *Music*, *American Life* and *Confessions on a Dance Floor* – promised something special. As the material-girl-turned-spiritual-girl celebrates her 60th birthday, she's still capable of stealing the show.

Opposite: Madonna shows that her flair for provocative fashion hasn't diminished at the Met Gala on May 7, 2018.

Above: Madonna poses with her son David, who spent 2017 training at the Benfica football academy in Portugal.

SOUNDTRACKS

Dressed as Eva Peron on the set
of *Evita*, in early 1996. To her right
is director Alan Parker.

CHAPTER 17
EVITA

Her sombre portrayal of Eva Peron in the 1996 film spawned the best-selling (11 million copies) soundtrack of her career. The Andrew Lloyd Webber/Tim Rice tunes are heavy going, but her voice never sounded stronger.

Looking not dissimilar to Eva Peron in
the video for 'Take a Bow'. The single
spent seven weeks at Number 1 in the UK.

EVITA

She lands the movie role of her life as Eva Peron, takes voice lessons so she'll be equal to the demands of the all-singing part and discovers a hitherto untapped part of her voice. Her newly uncovered abilities land her an Oscar and a Golden Globe.

The *Evita* album, released in November 1996, a month ahead of the film, contains a note from Madonna, thanking three people. In reverse order, they were: her personal manager, Caresse Henry-Norman; the film's musical director, David Caddick, who'd guided her through the process of singing with an orchestra; and vocal coach Joan Lader. To the last, she wrote: "Special thanks to Joan Lader for helping me find my voice". Lader came in for top honours because she had helped to expand her range, uncovering what Caddick described as "a bell-like purity". Having spent years being knocked for her voice's limitations, Madonna was thrilled to discover she had greater abilities than she'd dreamed.

She'd taken lessons from Lader because of the demands imposed by *Evita*. There was no dialogue in the movie – every line was sung, and she featured in 20 of the 31 songs. (Antonio Banderas, who played Che Guevara, had the second heaviest singing role, and possibly found it even more taxing, as he was singing in English and at a pace that was faster than he'd normally speak.) And the music fell outside her normal pop-dance parameters: the singers were backed by an 80-piece orchestra or, occasionally, just a bare-bones rhythm section. Added to that, Madonna had to act out the story while singing.

The film had been fitfully in the works since 1988. Inspired by Eva Peron's story – ambitious girl becomes controversial national icon – Madonna had tried to get the part then. She got as far as a meeting with *Evita*'s creator, Andrew Lloyd Webber, and Oliver Stone, who was then in the frame as director. She was, however, unsuccessful, and the role was offered to Meryl Streep. When Streep pulled out and Alan Parker was appointed director in 1995, Madonna lobbied him with a four-page letter that vowed she'd give it her all if he chose her.

He did, and she did. It was by far the most strenuous film she'd ever done. She was playing a controversial public figure – more than 40 years after Evita's death, emotions still ran high in Argentina among her supporters and detractors – and she was doing it on location, in Buenos Aires and Budapest. Moreover, she had to sing the entire role – and, halfway through, she discovered she was pregnant, which forced changes to the shooting schedule, so physically rigorous scenes were completed as quickly as possible. Yet it was eminently worth it: she won a Golden Globe for Best Actress and the film won an Oscar for Best Original Song (for 'You Must Love Me'). The film also picked up a Golden Globe for Best Picture – Comedy or Musical.

The recording of the album took place in London in October 1995, several months before filming began. (During filming, the actors mimed

> ## "Special thanks to Joan Lader for helping me find my voice."
>
> *Madonna*

Right: She acted out every scene in the recording studio, pulling Jimmy Nail around as they sang a scene together.

Far Right: The reward for her *Evita* exertions was the award for Best Actress at the 1997 Golden Globe Awards.

to the recorded music.) The studio sessions were also different from any she'd done before. She had no input with writing or production: the score, of course, had been composed by Lloyd Webber and Tim Rice (for their 1976 album-turned-musical), and it was produced by Lloyd Webber and Parker among others. According to Oliver Stone, Madonna had initially wanted to rewrite some of Webber's lyrics, an offer the composer had declined. Having said that, Lloyd Webber and Rice did go on to write a new song, the bittersweet 'You Must Love Me', specifically for the movie. The album sleeve does, however, credit Madonna with the technical role of mixing the album.

In the studio, like the other principal singers (Banderas, Geordie actor/pop star Jimmy Nail and Welsh actor Jonathan Pryce) Madonna sang with the full orchestra and then finished each track in a smaller studio with Parker and Caddick. Parker revealed that she was so intensely dedicated to getting to the core of Eva Peron that, while in the studio, she acted out each scene. During one song, she led Jimmy Nail around the room, going through the physical motions of the scene as they sang with hand microphones. Madonna herself told film critic Roger Ebert, "Then we got separated into different isolation booths and we could see each other through the Plexiglas and we were still acting the scenes out."

The resulting album was a full-scale rock opera, a genre that had last flourished in the 70s (with such albums as the Who's *Tommy* and Lloyd Webber and Rice's own *Jesus Christ Superstar*). And much of it

is more opera than rock: though some tracks are relatively catchy and sung in a conversational way, others are ponderous and slow-moving – sombre set pieces that need visuals in order to bring them to life. The opening 'Requiem for Evita', for example, is stirringly gloomy – four minutes of electric guitar and dramatic choir vocals – but not unique enough to work independently of the movie.

The three singles taken from the album do make decent standalone tracks. The biggest of them, the worldwide Top 10 hit 'Don't Cry for Me Argentina', has the regal quality of her most successful ballads, such as 'Live to Tell' or 'I'll Remember'. The Oscar-winning 'You Must Love Me' is quaveringly minimal: backed mainly by piano, Madonna was both plaintive and petulant, as required by the storyline. The final single, 'Another Suitcase in Another Hall', has the soundtrack stamp all over it, with other film characters murmuring in the background and a spectral horn section dipping in and out, but it was enough of a "Madonna" tune to peak at Number 7 in the UK.

Two songs, however – neither of them singles – are drenched with emotion that transcends genre. 'Your Little Body's Slowly Breaking Down', which accompanies the scene in which Evita learns she's dying, and Evita's dying 'Lament' are notably more poignant than anything else in the score. They were recorded live during filming – Parker decided to dispense with the pre-recorded versions because they didn't match the pathos of the scenes. Madonna's cracked, half-whispered performance on 'Lament' is a show-stopper. Parker revealed that even the film crew were in tears.

The soundtrack was released as two separate albums: the two-CD *Evita: the Complete Motion Picture Music Soundtrack* (containing the entire 107-minute score) and the single-disc, 17-track *Evita: Music from the Motion Picture*. As with the soundtracks for *Who's That Girl* and *I'm Breathless*, *Evita* was perceived as a Madonna album, which helped propel it up the chart. It reached Number 1 in the UK, Number 2 in the US and the Top 10 everywhere but Spain (where, perhaps, her portrayal of a Latin heroine didn't speak to consumers). The two releases sold a joint total of 11 million, thoroughly outstripping her two most recent studio albums, *Erotica* and *Bedtime Stories*.

Reviews of the film ranged from a rave in *Time* magazine to zero stars from the *Chicago Reader*, whose critic, Jonathan Rosenbaum, walked out halfway through. Madonna, he offered in mitigation, "fails honorably", but the music was "non-musical". By contrast, reviews of the soundtrack were more of a piece, praising Madonna's singing, but finding the album itself less engaging. Paul Du Noyer's assessment in *Q* magazine suggested that an appreciation of musicals in general was vital for listeners wanting to connect with the record.

Madonna, though, had the last laugh: if some reviews dismayed her, she needed only to glance at the mantelpiece where her Oscar and Golden Globe awards resided.

DISCOGRAPHY

ALBUMS

MADONNA // 1983

Lucky Star
Borderline
Burning Up
I Know It
Holiday
Think of Me
Physical Attraction
Everybody

**Bonus tracks
(2001 remastered edition)**
Burning Up (12" version)
Lucky Star
(previously unheard mix)

LIKE A VIRGIN // 1984

Material Girl
Angel
Like a Virgin
Over and Over
Love Don't Live Here Anymore
Into the Groove
Dress You Up
Shoo-Bee-Doo
Pretender
Stay

**Bonus tracks
(2001 remastered edition)**
Like a Virgin
(extended dance remix)
Material Girl
(extended dance remix)

TRUE BLUE // 1986

Papa Don't Preach
Open Your Heart
White Heat
Live to Tell
Where's the Party
True Blue
La Isla Bonita
Jimmy Jimmy
Love Makes the World Go Round

**Bonus tracks
(2001 remastered edition)**
True Blue (The Color Mix)
La Isla Bonita (extended remix)

LIKE A PRAYER // 1989

Like a Prayer
Express Yourself
Love Song
Till Death Do Us Part
Promise to Try
Cherish
Dear Jessie
Oh Father
Keep it Together
Spanish Eyes (known as *Pray for
Spanish Eyes* on some editions)
Act of Contrition

EROTICA // 1992

Erotica
Fever
Bye Bye Baby
Deeper and Deeper
Where Life Begins
Bad Girl
Waiting
Thief of Hearts
Words
Rain
Why's It So Hard
In This Life
Did You Do it?
(some editions only)
Secret Garden

BEDTIME STORIES // 1994

Survival
Secret
I'd Rather be Your Lover
Don't Stop
Inside of Me
Human Nature
Forbidden Love
Love Tried to Welcome Me
Sanctuary
Bedtime Story
Take a Bow

RAY OF LIGHT // 1998

Drowned World/ Substitute for Love
Swim
Ray of Light
Candy Perfume Girl
Skin
Nothing Really Matters
Sky Fits Heaven
Shanti/Ashtangi
Frozen
The Power of Good-bye
To Have and Not to Hold
Little Star
Mer Girl

MUSIC // 2000

Music
Impressive Instant
Runaway Lover
I Deserve It
Amazing
Nobody's Perfect
Don't Tell Me
What it Feels Like for a Girl
Paradise (Not for Me)
Gone
American Pie
(non-US editions only)

ALBUMS *CONTINUED...*

AMERICAN LIFE // 2003

American Life
Hollywood
I'm So Stupid
Love Profusion
Nobody Knows Me
Nothing Fails
Intervention
X-Static Process
Mother and Father
Die Another Day
Easy Ride

CONFESSIONS ON A DANCE FLOOR // 2005

Hung Up
Get Together
Sorry
Future Lovers
I Love New York
Let It Will Be
Forbidden Love
Jump
How High
Isaac
Push
Like It or Not
Fighting Spirit
(limited edition bonus track)
Super Pop
(limited edition bonus track)

HARD CANDY // 2008

Candy Shop
4 Minutes
Give it 2 Me
Heartbeat
Miles Away
She's Not Me
Incredible
Beat Goes On
Dance 2Night
Spanish Lesson
Devil Wouldn't Recognize You
Voices
Limited edition bonus tracks
4 Minutes (Tracy Mixshow Mix)
4 Minutes
(Peter Saves New York Mix)

MDNA // 2012

Girl Gone Wild
Gang Bang
I'm Addicted
Turn on the Radio
Give Me All Your Luvin'
Some Girls
Superstar
I Don't Give A
I'm a Sinner
Love Spent
Masterpiece
Falling Free
Deluxe edition bonus tracks
Beautiful Killer
I Fucked Up
B-Day Song
Best Friend
Give Me All Your Luvin'
(Party Rock Remix)

SOUNDTRACKS

REBEL HEART // 2015

Living for Love
Devil Pray
Ghosttown
Unapologetic Bitch
Illuminati
Bitch I'm Madonna
Hold Tight
Joan of Arc"
Iconic
HeartBreakCity
Body Shop
Holy Water
Inside Out
Wash All Over Me

WHO'S THAT GIRL // 1987

Who's That Girl
Causing a Commotion
The Look of Love
24 Hours (Duncan Faure)
Step by Step (Club Nouveau)
Turn it Up (Michael Davidson)
Best Thing Ever (Scritti Politti)
Can't Stop
El Coco Loco (So So Bad)
(Coati Mundi)

I'M BREATHLESS // 1990

He's a Man
Sooner or Later
Hanky Panky
I'm Going Bananas
Cry Baby
Something to Remember
Back in Business
More
What Can You Lose
Now I'm Following You (Part I)
Now I'm Following You (Part II)
Vogue

EVITA // 1996

Requiem for Evita
Oh What a Circus
On This Night of a Thousand Stars
*Eva and Magaldi/Eva Beware
  of the City*
Buenos Aires
Another Suitcase in Another Hall
Goodnight and Thank You
I'd be Surprisingly Good for You
Peron's Latest Flame
A New Argentina
Don't Cry for Me Argentina
High Flying, Adored
Rainbow High
*And the Money Kept Rolling in
  (and Out)*
She is a Diamond
Waltz for Eva and Che
You Must Love Me
Eva's Final Broadcast
Lament

SINGLES

Everybody **1982** [B-side: *Everybody* (instrumental)]

Burning Up **1983** *(Physical Attraction)*

Holiday **1983** (US: *I Know It*, UK: *Think of Me*)

Lucky Star **1983** *(I Know It)* (NB *I Know* It was used on both *Holiday* and *Lucky Star*)

Borderline **1984** (US: *Think of Me*, UK: *Physical Attraction* (edit))

Like a Virgin **1984** *(Stay)*

Material Girl **1984** *(Pretender)*

Crazy for You **1985** (US: *No More Words*, UK: *I'll Fall in Love Again*)

Angel **1985** (US: *Angel* (dance mix), UK: *Burning Up*)

Into the Groove **1985** (released outside US only) *(Shoo-Bee-Doo)*

Dress You Up **1985** (US: *Shoo-Bee-Doo*, UK: *I Know It*)

Gambler **1985** (released outside US only) *(Nature of the Beach)*

Live to Tell **1986** *(Live to Tell* (instrumental))

Papa Don't Preach **1986** *(Ain't No Big Deal)*

True Blue **1986** (US: *Ain't No Big Deal*, UK: *Holiday* (full-length version))

Open Your Heart **1987** (US: *White Heat*, UK: *Lucky Star* (edit))

La Isla Bonita **1987** *(La Isla Bonita* instrumental remix)

Who's That Girl **1989** (US: *Who's That Girl* (dub version), UK: *White Heat*)

Causing a Commotion **1987** *(Jimmy Jimmy)*

The Look of Love **1987** (released outside US only) *(I Know It /Love Don'tLive Here Anymore)*

Like a Prayer **1989** *(Act of Contrition)*

Express Yourself **1989** (US: *The Look of Love*, UK: *Express Yourself* (Stop & Go dubs))

Cherish **1989** *(Supernatural)*

Oh Father **1989** *(Pray for Spanish Eyes)*

Dear Jessie **1989** (released outside US only) *(Till Death Do Us Part)*

Keep it Together **1990** *(Keep it Together* (various mixes))

Vogue **1990** (US: *Vogue* (Bette Davis dub), UK: *Keep it Together* (single remix))

Hanky Panky **1990** *(More)*

Justify My Love **1990** *(Express Yourself 1990* (Shep's 'Spressin' Himself (Re-Remix))

Rescue Me **1991** (US: *Rescue Me* (alternate single mix), UK: *Spotlight*)

This Used To Be My Playground **1992** *(This Used to be My Playground* (long version))

Erotica **1992** *(Erotica* (instrumental))

Deeper and Deeper **1992** *(Deeper and Deeper* (various mixes))

Bad Girl **1993** (US: *Fever*, UK: *Erotica* (William Orbit Dub))

Fever **1993** (released outside US only) *(Fever* (Murk Boys Radio Edit))

Rain **1993** (US: *Waiting*, UK: *Open Your Heart*)

Bye Bye Baby **1993** (released outside US only) *(Bye Bye Baby* (various mixes))

I'll Remember **1994** (US: *Secret Garden*, UK: *I'll Remember* (Orbit Remix))

Secret **1994** *(Let Down Your Guard)*

Take a Bow **1994** (US: *Take a Bow* (various mixes))

Bedtime Story **1995** (US: *Survival*, UK: *Secret* (Allstar Mix))

Human Nature **1995** (US: *Sanctuary*, UK: *Human Nature* (Human Club Mix))

You'll See **1995** (US: *You'll See* (instrumental), UK: *Rain* (album version))

One More Chance **1996** *(You'll See* (Spanish version))

Love Don't Live Here Anymore **1996** *(Do It, Do It)*

You Must Love Me **1996** *(Rainbow High)*

Don't Cry for Me Argentina **1996** (US: *Don't Cry for Me Argentina* (Miami Spanglish Mix), UK: *Santa Evita/Latin Chant*)

Another Suitcase in Another Hall **1997** *(Don't Cry for Me Argentina* (Miami Mix Edit))

Frozen **1998** (US: *Shanti/Ashtangi*, UK: *Frozen* (Stereo MCs Remix))

Ray of Light **1998** (US: *Ray of Light* (Orbit's Ultraviolet Mix), UK: *Has to Be*)

Drowned World/ Substitute for Love **1998** (released outside US only) *(Sky Fits Heaven)*

The Power of Good-bye **1998** (US: *Mer Girl*, UK: *Little Star*)

Nothing Really Matters **1999** (US: *To Have and Not to Hold*, UK: **Nothing Really Matters** *(Club 69 Radio Mix))

Beautiful Stranger **1999** (released outside US only) *(Beautiful Stranger* (Calderone Radio Mix))

American Pie **2000** *(American Pie* (Victor Calderone Filter Dub Mix))

Music **2000** (US: *Cyber-Raga*, UK: *Music* (various remixes))

Don't Tell Me **2000** *(Don't Tell Me* (Thunderpuss's 2001 Hands in the Air Mix), UK: *Cyber-Raga*)

What it Feels Like for a Girl **2001** *(What it Feels Like for a Girl* (various mixes))

Die Another Day **2002** *(Die Another Day* (various mixes))

American Life **2003** *(American Life* (various mixes))

Hollywood **2003** *(Hollywood* (various mixes))

Nothing Fails **2003** *(Nothing Fails* (various mixes))

Love Profusion **2003** (US: *Love Profusion* (various mixes), UK: *Nothing Fails* (radio edit))

Hung Up **2005** *(Hung Up* (various mixes))

Sorry **2006** (US: *Sorry* (various mixes), UK: *Let it Will Be*)

Get Together **2006** *(Get Together* (various mixes))

Jump **2006** *(Jump* (various mixes), *History*)

4 Minutes **2008** *(4 Minutes* (various mixes))

Give it 2 Me **2008** *(Give it to Me* (various mixes))

Miles Away **2008** *(Miles Away* (various mixes))

Celebration **2009** *(Celebration* (various mixes))

Revolver **2009** *(Celebration* remix feat Akon)

Give Me All Your Luvin' **2012** *(Give Me All Your Luvin'* (various mixes))

Girl Gone Wild **2012** *(Girl Gone Wild* (various mixes))

Turn Up the Radio **2012** *(Turn Up the Radio* (various mixes))

Right: Who is that girl? The Queen of Pop in her imperial phase, Montreal, July 1987.

INDEX

CREDITS

BIBLIOGRAPHY

BOOKS

Bordo, Susan. "Material Girl: Madonna as Postmodern Heroine". In *The Fashion Reader*, 2d ed, edited by Linda Welters and Abby Lillethun. BERG, 2011.

Ciccone, Christopher and Leigh, Wendy. *Life with My Sister Madonna*. Pocket Books, 2009.

Clifton, Keith. "Queer Hearing and the Madonna queen." In *Madonna's Drowned Worlds: New Approaches to Her Cultural Transformations*, edited by Santiago Fouz-Hernandez and Freya Jarman-Ivens, pp 55–68. Ashgate Publishing Limited, 2004.

Fouz-Hernandez, Santiago and Jarman-Ivens, Freya, ed. *Madonna's Drowned Worlds: New Approaches to Her Cultural Transformations*. Ashgate Publishing Limited, 2004.

Gutman, Tara. *Talking Up: Young Women's Take on Feminism*. Edited by Naomi Flutter and Rosamund Else-Mitchell. Spinifex Press, 2003.

Nice, James. *Shadowplayers: The Rise and Fall of Factory Records*. Aurum Press, 2011.

O'Brien, Lucy. *Madonna: Like an Icon*. Corgi, 2008.

Parker, Alan. *The Making of Evita*. HarperSanFrancisco, 1996.

Taraborrelli, J. Randy. *Madonna: An Intimate Biography*. Pan, 2008.

Vickers, Nancy J. "Maternalism and the Material Girl." In *Embodied Voices: Representing Female Vocality in Western Culture*, edited by Nancy Jones and Leslie C. Dunn. Cambridge University Press, 1996.

Zeisler, Andi. *Feminism and Pop Culture*. Avalon Publishing Group, 2008

MAGAZINES

INTRODUCTION
Rolling Stone • Sean Howe • Austin Scaggs

CHAPTER 1
The Advocate • Don Shewey • 1991
Los Angeles Times • Robert Hilburn • 1984

CHAPTER 2
The Atlantic • Chris Williams
The Face
Hollywood Reporter • 2013
Rolling Stone
AllMusic.com
MadonnaTribe.com
The Quietus

CHAPTER 3
Atlanta Journal-Constitution • Mary Edgar Smith
Billboard
Blender
Chicago Sun Times • Roger Ebert
Clash • Mike Diver • 2013
New York Times • Stephen Holden • Vincent Canby
Slant
Smash Hits • 1984
Variety
AllMusic.com

CHAPTER 4
Daily Telegraph • Isabel Albiston
Edge Boston • Phil Hall
Entertainment Weekly • David Browne
Madonna Tribe.com
Los Angeles Times • Robert Hilburn • Sheila Benson

New York Times • Stephen Holden
Rolling Stone • Sigerson, Davitt
San Francisco Chronicle • Peter Stack
Slant • Sal Cinquemani
SputnikMusic.com • Frederick Metzengerstein *Variety*
Vanity Fair: December 1986 • Michael Gross
Vogue • Bruce Handy

CHAPTER 5
America: The National Catholic Review • The Rev. Andrew M. Greeley
Austin American-Statesman • Kevin Philly
Cox News Service • Phil Kloer
Daily News • Howard Kissell
Gawker • Richard Juzwiak • 2012
Knight Ridder • David Rosenthal
Los Angeles Daily News • Bruce Britt
New York Times • Frank Rich
Philadelphia Inquirer quotes Bob Garfield
Rolling Stone • Bill Zehme • J. D. Considine
Smash Hits • Chris Heath
Trouser Press • Natasha Stovall, Ira Robbins, Brad Reno • 2008
Vanity Fair • 1991 • Lynn Hirschberg

CHAPTER 6
AVClub.com • 2002
Baltimore Sun • J. D. Considine
Chicago Tribune • Gene Siskel
Daily Telegraph • Neil McCormick • 2014
Deseret News • Chris Hicks
Entertainment Weekly • Giselle Benatar • David Browne
Hartford Courant • Roger Catlin
Independent • Zoe Heller
New York magazine • Michael Gross
New York Times • Vicki Goldberg • Jon Pareles
Newsweek • John Leland
Rolling Stone • Arion Berger
Stylus • Alfred Soto • 2006
Vanity Fair • Maureen Orth
Variety • two references, one David Stratton

CHAPTER 7
Attitude
Buzz
Entertainment Weekly • Jim Farber
Los Angeles Times • Chris Willman
Rolling Stone • Barbara O'Dair
Spin • Bob Guccione Jr • 1995

CHAPTER 8
Keyboard • Greg Rule
People • Todd Gold
Rolling Stone • Rob Sheffield
Vanity Fair • Kevin Sessums
Washington Post • Martha Sherrill • 1991
Yediot Ahronot • Madonna • 2009

CHAPTER 9
Spin • Bob Guccione • 1996
NME
Observer • Simon Garfield
Allmusic.com • Stephen Thomas Erlewine
Vibe • Dimitri Ehrlich
The Face • Miranda Sawyer
Guardian • Gary Mulholland
Georgia Straight • Craig Takeuchi
Spin magazine • Alex Pappademas
New York magazine • Ethan Brown
Pop Heaven website
NME
PopMatters.com • Eden Miller

CHAPTER 10
Guardian • Alexis Petridis
Village Voice • Jessica Winter
Stylus magazine, stylusmagazine.com • Ed Howard
Blender magazine
Guy Penn and the Gospel According to Madge, guypenn.com
Slant magazine, slantmagazine.com
Q magazine • Paul Rees
Newsday • John Anderson
Guardian • Michael Billington
Theatre World, theatreworldinternetmagazine.com • Philip Fisher
PopDust.com • Andrew Unterberger

CHAPTER 11
Attitude magazine • Matthew Todd
Observer • Kate Kellaway
US *Vogue*, August 2005 •
Observer • Simon Garfield
Observer • Peter Robinson
BBC • Alan Braidwood
Austin Chronicle • Margaret Moser
Pitchfork, pitchfork.com • Stephen M Deusner
New York magazine • Ben Williams
Village Voice • Joan Morgan

CHAPTER 12
Village Voice • Robert Christgau
Sunday Telegraph • Jonathon Moran
Vanity Fair
Boston Globe • Joan Anderman
Prefix magazine • Dan Nishimoto
AVClub.com • Andy Battaglia

CHAPTER 13
NME • Priya Elan
New York Post • Mandy Stadtmiller
Daily Mail • Baz Bamigboye
Guardian • Michael Cragg
Guardian • Caroline Sullivan
Independent • Andy Gill
Complex
Q magazine • Simon Goddard
Guardian • Alexis Petridis

CHAPTER 14
Guardian • Sophie Heawood, Alexis Petridis, Arundel XVI
Billboard • Keith Caulfield
Salon.com
Playboy
Idolator.com • Kathy Iandolf
Daily Telegraph • Neil McCormick
TheQuietus.com • Amy Pettifer
Spin.com
AVClub.com • Annie Zaleski
Daily News • Jim Farber
Boston Globe • James Reed

CHAPTER 15
Spin magazine • 1988
New York magazine • David Denby

CHAPTER 16
Newsweek magazine • David Ansen
Q magazine

CHAPTER 17
Newsweek • David Ansen
Time
Chicago Reader • Jonathan Rosenbaum
Baltimore Sun
Q magazine • Paul du Noyer